SHORT, SWEET, & UPLIFTING

72 POSITIVE AND INSPIRATIONAL STORIES THAT WILL MAKE YOU BELIEVE IN HUMANITY

CHARLIE MILLER

ISBN: 978-1-64845-122-5

CONTENTS

INTRODUCTION

Welcome to this book of positivity, uplifting tales and reasons to smile. Relax, this is a nice book. The stories have been selected with the specific aim of making you—that's right *you*—feel like the world can be cheery.

If you pay attention to the news, which you should if you don't, then you will be beset with negativity. This will only be compounded if you're on social media regularly—most of us are and probably shouldn't be—as that brings an extra sprinkling of misinformation as well. Add that to a busy work life, family obligations, arguments, and money worries…well, it is easy to feel like life's a bit miserable. The main reason we focus so much on negatives is that they often seem more urgent; they're the political disasters, ecological problems, and other world events that affect all of us.

It's also often easier to be entertained by negatives. Many movies and TV shows rely on it. How many comedy shows are laughing at the characters failing, rather than succeeding? Horror movies are entirely built around misery, horror, and anger. Stories that are about negative experiences afford a certain amount of *schadenfreude*, and we like that itch to be scratched when we look at others' misfortune. Watching someone slip over a puddle or fail to profit from an immoral business enterprise is quite pleasant and may very well make you smile. However, we don't *only* have to pay attention to the negatives to be entertained in life. The world is full of magic, mystery, and smiles—we just have to look carefully to find them sometimes.

Most of the following 72 stories are modern ones from the 21st century (though there are some historical ones as well). The 21st century, after all, is the one you're in and likely is the one that is making you desire a bit of cheering up. (Unless you're reading this from a future century, in which case, fantastic! With any luck, Earth's doing well. If it isn't, then I truly hope that Mars is okay.)

You'll find news of individuals making great personal sacrifices to help others, countries working hard to help save the planet, and a story about Morgan Freeman's bee obsession. Regardless of their topic, they're objectively smile-worthy tales and one should feel a flurry of joy while reading. If you find that this doesn't happen, and instead you're taken with a spiking of rage and frustration, then the problem may lie somewhere deeper than this book.

The stories are also all true. There is no reliance on speculation or overzealous exaggeration. The writing has to be true; otherwise, a true antidote to life's upsets isn't being offered. This is no peddling of snake oil. This is the real thing; an actual cure for "being a bit bummed out because the world's tough.". Enjoy the stories, take something away from them, and if you *really* like the

2

book, allow yourself to be helped by them. See the world more lightly, smile at the sky more, and leave five-star reviews on Amazon for this collection of stories that made you smile.

USING WHAT
THEY GAVE YOU

Motivation can be hard to come by when you're in a difficult, or sometimes hopeless, position. That "hopeless position" can really be anything. It's perfectly normal to feel a bit like you've lost all hope and when you feel that way, it's difficult to motivate yourself out of that. One may think of times when they, or a relative, have been very sick or a period of life where you've been without consistent employment, staring down the barrel of a temporary lack of funding. A scenario that you're *unlikely* to find yourself in, however, is facing a 28-year-long prison sentence for a crime that you know full well you didn't commit.

This was the *hopeless* scenario facing Jarrett Adams in 1998 when he was arrested under the accusation of sexual assault. The court provided Adams with a public defendant, as was his right, due to his inability to afford one himself. The lawyer advised Adams not to put a defense in front of the judge at all.

"We know you didn't do it...The best defense is a no-defense strategy."

In the end, the public defendant's inability to be proactive by calling on a witness who could corroborate Adams' timeline of events, left Adams with a 28-year prison sentence and all signs of a future or prosperity shut down. Adams began his sentence, every last swig of motivation inside of him draining away by the day. Then he met a man who worked in the prison law library.

The inmate told Adams that he was confident of Adams' innocence. He claimed that every prisoner says they're innocent, but he was sure that Adams was and that he should do his best to prove it—*quickly.*

> *"It's only going to take a second before you have tattoos on your face and have given up and completely don't care at all. You need to go down swinging."*

Adams worked tirelessly to clear his name, searching for all precedents that could exonerate him. He was confident that he could prove that the court failed to provide him with effective counsel in this case and so doomed him to failure before a jury even stepped foot inside the courtroom. Adams reached out to the Wisconsin Innocence Project, a nonprofit devoted to freeing wrongfully convicted people. They agreed to help Adams.

Adams was freed in 2007, after spending almost a full decade in prison, and he enrolled in community college the same year. In 2015, he graduated from law school and gained employment with the Wisconsin Innocence Project, as he sought to make sure that other innocent prisoners were provided with the chance for freedom when they deserved it. Adams continues to work for the project in the 2020s, even returning to the very courtroom that sentenced him to 28 years, to prove the innocence of a prisoner while being addressed as "Attorney Adams."

SAVING LIVES IS
WHAT'S TRULY BADASS

You may have either lived under a small rock for the last 30 years or have largely dismissed news concerning any well-known celebrities. If either of these, is you, then you may not know who Keanu Reeves is.

Keanu Reeves is a world-famous actor who has starred in several huge movies and franchises such as *The Matrix Movies, John Wick 1-4*, and *Bram Stoker's Dracula*. He is worth a reported $400 million and continues to be cast in major motion pictures regularly. He is also recognized for two other reasons: firstly, it's rumored that Keanu Reeves is a vampire as he doesn't seem to age, and secondly, Reeves is known for being a genuinely nice person.

Reeves had a tough childhood, with a lack of stability in his family due to several divorces and marriages and his attendance at four different high schools. His mother educated Reeves in English manners from an early age, something that he has pointed to as influencing him throughout his life. He faced great grief later in his life as well, from the loss of his partner to his sister's diagnosis and battle with cancer.

In 2009, It came to light that throughout the 2000s, Reeves was secretly financing several charities and children's hospitals. Due to his sister's connection with the disease, he has donated funds to many cancer charities and established his own charitable foundation. Reeves has publicly said he is very proud of the work that they do but refuses to attach his name to the project. Reeves states that the foundation is funded by him, but the people doing the good work there should be left to do that work alone without interest because of his name.

Anecdotal stories have emerged from film sets about Reeves' charitable doings there as well. He reportedly paid for free meals for the stagehands and workers of *The Matrix* as well as providing one worker facing financial difficulties with $20,000. During the filming of *Matrix Reloaded*, he bought every member of the special effects team a Harley-Davidson motorcycle to thank them for their work. He gifted the stunt team from *John Wick 4*, Rolex watches for their contributions.

Yes, this story reads like a press release from his publicist, so let's put it into context. The story of Reeves is not isolated; many celebrities are charitable and use their status to do good in the world. But what makes his case interesting is that he doesn't publicize much of his work. Instead, Reeves chooses to help without feeling the need to talk too much about it. His reasoning, according to a family friend, is that he's embarrassed at his level of fortune and finds it morally incorrect to hoard it for himself…

By the way, no pressure—you don't have to exact the same level of charity!

NOT EVERYTHING
IS FOR SALE

It's always refreshing to see the little man win. To see an individual or small group stand up for what is right, for their own liberties, or just so that someone is, is always inspiring. It's even better when the small group stands up to a large, powerful body such as a company or government. Perhaps this brings to mind *The Tank Man*, a photo publicized in 1989, showing a protestor in China standing in front of a long line of tanks. He momentarily halted their progress toward suppressing a student protest, producing a startling single frame of defiance and assuredness. Seeing the little man win, even if for just a minute, lights a small fire in the chest of many of us.

In 2019, the Ecuadorian government found themselves on the receiving end of this single-minded determination when they lost a court battle against the indigenous Waorani communities that live in the Amazon Rainforest, in Ecuador.

The government wanted to sell off about seven million acres of land in the rainforest for companies to drill for oil. Ecuador is experiencing slow economic growth and finds itself swamped in debt. The government's intentions were, of course, to begin exploratory drilling for oil so that they could begin to chip away at the mountain of accumulated debt.

The Waorani people took the government to court. The rainforest is home to dozens of communities whose lives would be uprooted by the destruction of the natural surroundings in favor of oil extraction. Plus, they wanted to highlight the environmental impact of clearing such a vast amount of the world's largest rainforest. The court found in the indigenous people's favor, ruling that the sale of the land without their consent would be illegal.

The Waorani people's victory is a monumental moment for indigenous people's rights, especially for those who live in the Amazon rainforest, which has been subject to massive amounts of deforestation over the last century. Members of the Waorani took to the streets of Puyo to celebrate the court's decision, which was also celebrated globally. The Ecuadorian government plans on bringing the case before different courts, in an attempt to change the verdict, but the Waorani people have made it clear that if they have to, they'll bring the debacle to the attention of worldwide courts to prevent their land from being surrendered to greed.

WHO NEEDS ANOTHER BILLIONAIRE ANYWAY?

Patagonia is a successful outdoor clothing brand that has gained a trustworthy reputation as a producer of high-quality products that come with a relatively hefty price tag. Owner Yvon Chouinard set the company up in the 1980s and then in 2022, Patagonia held a valuation of approximately $3 billion. The owner is an exceptionally wealthy man, as is his family, due to the success and standards of the company. In September 2022, Chouinard laid a gauntlet down for every successful business owner in the age of the global climate crisis.

Chouinard wrote an open letter, published on the company's website, announcing that he was giving away the company, and its future profits, to fight worsening climate change. The company's aesthetic and design drew heavy inspiration from South America's wilderness, and Chouinard wants to do all he can to help protect it.

The company makes approximately $100m per year in profit, after paying a fair wage to its employees and taxes on its income. Chouinard, along with his family, decided that this figure could do a great deal of good for the world rather than lining the pockets of an already wealthy family. Chouinard announced that 2% of the company would go to a newly established trust called the Patagonia Purpose Trust, which is run by members of his family and close advisors. The trust exists to ensure that the company sticks to its promise as time goes by.

The remaining 98% of the company was then given to the non-profit organization, Holdfast Collective, which will directly receive all profits made by Patagonia. The Holdfast Collective will directly use that profit to fund projects around the world aimed at fighting worsening climate change.

Chouinard will continue to work as a philanthropist, as he has done for much of his life, though will not take any income from Patagonia. In fact, he paid the $17.5 million bill in taxes that came from handing the company over. In 2023, *TIME* magazine voted him as one of the 100 most influential people in the world for his activism and generosity.

So even if the t-shirts cost approximately $50, if you decide to purchase one, you can sleep happily knowing that your money could be helping safeguard the world for future generations.

I'M GOING TO GO
AND DO MY LAUNDRY...

You know all those useless bits of paper and detritus that build up over the weeks, months, and years? The stacks of receipts, invoices, wedding invitations, birthday cards, candy wrappers, and useless *stuff*. Well, it may be prudent to occasionally go through some of that. There may be something worthwhile in there that you've taken your eye off of. That's what pensioner Jimmie Smith thought in 2017 when he decided to check the pockets of an old shirt into which he'd stuffed various bits and bobs.

Smith is a now-retired security officer and was enjoying his new, quieter life when an urgent message was broadcast by Gweneth Dean, director of the Commission's Division of the Lottery.

"We urge New York Lottery players: Check your pockets. Check your glove box. Look under the couch cushions. If you have this winning ticket, we look forward to meeting you."

The New York Gaming Commission was looking for a lottery winner from May 25, 2016. Winners have one year to claim their ticket to receive a payout, and the date of the director's message was May 23, 2017, so it was one last appeal to see if the lucky winner could be reached.

Well, 68-year-old Smith knew that in those old shirt pockets existed several lottery tickets that he'd bought and stored. Doubting that he would be such a lucky man, Smith leafed through the lottery tickets before landing on the one dated May 25, 2016. He scanned the numbers:

05 – 12 – 13 – 22 – 25 – 35

He'd won! Smith says that he was in utter shock, having to stick his head out of the window to catch some fresh air before rechecking the ticket about a hundred times before he could believe it. Smith called up to claim his winnings a mere 48 hours before he would have been ineligible to, and the New York Lottery happily announced the winner and recipient of $24.1 million to be Jimmie Smith.

Smith chose to receive his winnings spread out over 26 years, thus providing a small increase to his pension. He said there'd have to be an "all-family discussion" to consider his new fortune. Either he'll have pledged to start college funds for all children, alongside help with mortgages for all, and charitable donations—or he'll have said, "Get stuffed, I never want to see you again! I'm going to go and live in Hawaii to kick-start my hobby of cigar-smoking and poker playing." Either way, good luck to you, Jimmie. Hopefully, we all get to enjoy retirement as much as you will.

HOW NOT TO LET THE BULLIES GET TO YOU

Whether you're an adult, child, or in-between, a fact of life is that *kids are cruel*. Parents lament children's ability to tell the blunt truth to their faces, regardless of whether it hurts their feelings or not:

"You've put on weight, Dad."

"You're not as funny as you think you are, you know."

"You've gotten really old."

The truth is that though kids can be cruel to adults as they don't yet understand the nuances of social politeness or grace, kids are crueler still to other kids. No matter the strategies that are put in place by schools to combat bullying, children across the world experience bullying that can severely affect their happiness for years to come. British pupil 13-year-old Nadia Sparkes experienced the blunt end of this in 2019 when she faced harsh bullying because she cared for the local community.

Nadia would leave her house for school one hour early every day so that she had the time to pick litter before her classes began. She also donated her time to do this more often on non-school days. It's the sort of act that a reasonable adult looks at with a smile, grateful for the volunteered charity from a young teenager. Some would go so far as to say that her actions are inspiring.

Unfortunately, a select few pupils at her high school didn't see it that way, for one reason or another. Nadia experienced vicious bullying and was dubbed "Trash Girl" by the unhappy children who saw it as their job to pick on her. She once had to sit through an entire lesson drenched in orange juice that had been poured on her. In an especially serious incident, she was chased and beaten by a pupil brandishing a knife. This incident was the last straw for her mother, and the Norfolk police force became involved, with one bully referred to the Youth Offending Team.

Nadia's story gained national attention, including masses of online support for her charitable work, and she decided to turn the rude nickname into a positive.

"I'm not going to stop doing the right thing because of them and if they are going to call me trash girl, they can say it with respect. I'm doing something to protect the world they also live in."

Nadia has since found a new school that actively supports her care for the community and she was awarded, along with a green-fingered teacher who champions her, the Points of Light award by then-Prime Minister Theresa May. May wrote to Nadia to express her gratitude to Nadia for being a positive role model for British people to care for their environment.

Nadia continues to volunteer her time to care for the environment, still operating under the name Trash Girl.

Hopefully, the bullies have since had enough distance and time to grow up and join Team Trash.

AN ENGLISHMAN WALKS
INTO A BAR AND WITHDRAWS
PLANNING PERMISSION

Did you know that in 2019, the United Kingdom had more than 47,000 pubs? The pub, or public house, is a staple of UK culture and is the third-most popular activity for tourists in the country. Pubs are shown to encourage a sense of community, provide adult social spaces, and allow 20-year-olds to over-drink before throwing up in the street. They remain an important consistent in British society, with some pubs dating back to the 11th century CE and a large number predating the founding of America. Yet public house numbers have been on the decline, with a reported 25% of pubs that have closed their doors permanently in the 21st century.

The closure of a pub is often a sad moment for communities in the UK. Unless the pub was awful, in which case the news of closure is shrugged at, followed by a remark such as, "the Red Lion is a better pub, anyway". But generally speaking, it's a loss. There are many reasons for pub closures, including higher taxes on alcohol, lower drinking rates among young people, and smoking bans. But it leaves landowners desperate to do something with a pleasant building that no longer operates as a business, so they either destroy or convert the building to make flats.

This was the case with the Carlton Tavern in West London when it closed its doors in April 2015. The owners had requested planning permission to convert the large pub into ten flats, which would likely have brought a massive amount of money in for the landowners. This request was denied, and they were informed that Historic England would be coming to look at the building to decide if it should be a listed building. In the UK, a listed building holds historical significance or is of a certain age and so requires special consideration for modern alterations.

Two days before the visit, the owners demolished the Carlton Tavern. Thousands of locals were furious at the decision and implored the local council to intervene, which they did. Westminster council informed CTLX, the owners, to rebuild the Carlton Tavern brick-by-brick. The order further stipulated that the building would have to look the same, using the same materials. This meant the same bricks, the same style of building and even the same sign proudly displaying the name.

CTLX said that this would be impossible to do but luckily, help was provided by Historic England, who had already visited the pub before the demolition and had taken meticulous pictures of the site and a plaster cast of every tile. Thus, there was a perfectly detailed plan given to the landowners so that they could properly rebuild the ancient pub. The pub now has new owners who look to maintain it and work to ensure it stays as it always has done, much to the delight of its thousands of loyal patrons.

Don't come between an Englishman and his pint!

HOW TO TACKLE HATE

"What I have come to find to be the greatest and most effective and successful weapon that we can use, known to man, to combat such adversaries as ignorance, racism, hatred, violence, is also the least expensive weapon, and the one that is the least used by Americans. That weapon is called communication."

Humans have had a problem with hatred and disrespect for the entirety of our history. Notable examples include millennium-long antisemitism, the African slave trade, and waves of fascism in the early 20th century. In other words, hatred is nothing new, but most would believe that, in the 21st century, society is probably more tolerant and nicer than it has been before. In the 20th century, however, America found itself on the back foot due to its harsh race laws around segregation, leading to some serious problems with racism that persist to this day.

One example of this unacceptable racism was the hate group the Ku Klux Klan (KKK), which gained notoriety for its violence and terrorist acts against Black people. Up until the 1960s, the KKK seemed to have *carte blanche* to do whatever they wanted with minimum repercussions. The group still operates today but represents a very small and confused section of society. So, bearing in mind their violence, murder, and terrorizing of Black people, you'd have to be a particularly brave individual to engage with them to convince them to stop being racist.

This is what famous African-American musician Daryl Davis (quoted above) has done since the 1980s. It started in 1983 when Daryl Davis was playing the piano in a supposed "White" bar in Maryland. A man approached Davis and told him that he'd "never heard a black man play as well as Jerry Lee Lewis," to which Davis informed him that Jerry Lee Lewis was actually taught by Black piano players and was a personal friend of his. The men chatted before the patron disclosed that he was a member of the KKK. Davis didn't run away, nor ridicule him. Instead, they had a drink, exchanged contact information, and started a friendship.

The interaction inspired Davis. The man had left behind some serious prejudices by forming a friendship with Davis, all by just having a chat. Could Davis do it again? He procured the contact information of Klan leaders from his new friend and set to work.

Davis has gone on to engage directly with Klan members ever since and has helped many find their way out of the organization. He famously met with the Imperial Wizard of the Maryland branch of the KKK, concealing his race before the meeting. Supposedly the meeting started tensely but ended with Davis being gifted with the leader's robe as well as being asked to be his daughter's godfather.

Davis remains friends with 20 former Klan members and claims to have directly, or indirectly, caused more than 200 people to leave the hate group. He's been gifted over 25 robes from members and leaders, as well as a gold medallion holding the inscription "KKK-member in good standing." He has been present for ex-members' weddings and funerals while starting his own social media platform, Minds, which aims to promote real and meaningful conversations between people with different points of view.

Davis is an inspirational figure because he was willing to just talk to people he didn't agree with. Many of us could take a leaf out of his book in our increasingly polarized world. Rather than shirk away from the person who irritates you, perhaps it's worth trying to understand them first.

STANDING AGAINST
TOTAL EVIL

In the depths of humanity's worst tale, World War II, several stories have emerged over the years to show us that it didn't all just fall apart. In Europe, Nazi Germany was dominant for years and began its hunt for Jewish people with the sole aim of erasing them from the face of the earth. The speed of the Nazis' advances made attempts to flee or hide very difficult. The Nazis used *blitzkrieg* tactics and rapid aggression that forced nations to fall under their control. Jewish people who couldn't flee or hide faced murder, torture, and concentration camps. The Nazis encouraged civilians to inform on any Jewish people and threatened collaborators or resistors with death.

But there were many resistors. Many people refused to bow down to fascism and mindless brutality. Famously, the Frank family spent years hiding in an attic in Amsterdam, Netherlands before being captured in 1945 (all documented in *The Diary of Anne Frank*). Their story is historically revealing, helping us understand the terror involved in desperately hiding from the unstoppable evil that was the Nazis. Other stories convey the bravery of those who offered to assist Jewish people as well, risking everything when they didn't have to. One especially impressive individual was Corrie ten Boom.

Corrie was a watchmaker and a Christian from the Netherlands. The ten Boom family was successful and lived a comfortable life in pre-war Europe. Her brother was a Christian minister who studied European antisemitism, something that was championed by her grandfather who had spent time in the 19th century trying to improve Christian-Jewish relations in Europe. Corrie was a beloved member of the community in *Haarlem*. Her Christian belief told her to be kind to everyone—she knew Jewish people were precious to God and that he viewed everyone equally.

So, when a Jewish woman came to her home in 1942, suitcase in hand, and informed Corrie that the Nazis had taken her husband and she feared for her life, Corrie brought her into her home. Thus began the ten Boom's involvement in the Dutch Resistance, an underground movement that acted against the Nazis in the Netherlands. The family welcomed Jewish people in, providing them with food, shelter, and an escape route out. The Resistance helped establish a secret hiding place for Jews in the ten Boom's home, provided extra food rations, and worked with the family.

It's estimated that the family's work saved 800 Jewish people during World War II. They were captured by the Nazis in 1944, and Corrie was brought to a concentration camp with her sister, who died there. Due to a clerical error, Corrie was released in

December 1944 — the group she had been imprisoned with was executed less than two weeks later.

Corrie went on to spend the rest of her life devoted to charitable acts in the name of God, never seeking to convert but instead to help. She died on her 91st birthday in 1983, with her memoirs having been published and a movie made telling the incredible story of how she stood up for those whose voice had been taken away.

MUHAMMED ALI THE LIFE-SAVING FIGHTER

If you ask most people to name a boxer, they'll give you one of three answers: Rocky Balboa, the Marquess of Queensbury, or Muhammed Ali.

Muhammed Ali remains one of the most decorated athletes of all time with medals and awards galore. He fought at a time when Black people weren't valued as equally as White people in America, yet he was politically outspoken, advocating for equality for all and criticizing the war. Though he spent his career beating people up, Ali is well remembered for his charming personality, dazzling confidence, and gentle nature. One man called Joe, who may well be alive today, will remember Ali for saving his life on January 19, 1981.

Joe was a veteran of the Vietnam War and had lost his way since returning from the conflict. He saw little to live for and decided to commit suicide. He took himself to the ninth floor of an office building, attempting to build up the courage to take his life. A crowd gathered made up of bystanders, police officers, and one photographer from the *Los Angeles Times* called Boris Yaro. The scene was unpleasant. One young man who desperately needed help was being goaded and laughed at by unconcerned Los

Angeles pedestrians, with officers encouraging him to come down, helplessly wondering if they'll see a man die today or not.

Joe was there for hours. Luckily for him, a man called Howard Bingham was in the crowd. Bingham was a close friend of Muhammed Ali, and he thought that given Ali's outspoken advocacy for veterans and support from the Black communities of America, he might be able to help. He phoned Ali, who lived nearby.

A Rolls Royce careered up the street, on the wrong side of the road, with its lights blinking desperately warning people to get out of the way! A life needed saving! Ali leaped from the vehicle and dashed into the building, finding his way to the ninth floor, where he walked through an office to a window. He leaned out and stared at Joe.

Joe looked back at Ali, almost losing his footing in the process, presumably absolutely dumbfounded by who he saw. Ali shouted to him,

"You're my brother! I love you, and I couldn't lie to you."

Ali ran through to the fire escape and embraced Joe, bringing him inside. Ali brought him to his car (just another part of his day that Joe would have struggled to fully comprehend) and drove to the hospital. If it wasn't for Boris Yaro, the photographer, then this story might have been lost to the annuls of history and faded as a tale of doubt and "probably didn't happen." But Yaro snapped images of Ali talking to Joe and if you Google it, you will see the face of the world's greatest fighter saving the life of someone who he'd never met but felt implored to help.

THE WRESTLER WITH BIG BICEPS, AND AN EVEN BIGGER HEART

Wrestling is a cornerstone of entertainment sports worldwide. It features big muscly people throwing each other around in a remarkable display of athletics and an even more remarkable display of atrocious acting. Being a pro athlete leads you to have fans, and those fans will look up to you. For wrestlers, this can be tricky to manage as they usually focus their stage persona on being "tough" and ready for a bout of fighting at a moment's notice. So how do you make sure that you are a positive role model to the world's youth without ruining your wrestling career?

The famous WWE wrestler John Cena has expertly shown, over the last 20 years or so, how one does this. John Cena currently holds the Guinness World Record for the most Make-a-Wish wishes granted. The Make-a-Wish Foundation is a charity that grants children who are suffering from a terminal illness their wish. It's normally something that one would struggle to make happen in normal circumstances, either due to financial restrictions or improbability. Common wishes include swimming with dolphins, Disneyland tickets, travel, or meeting John Cena.

In September 2022, John Cena had his 650th wish ratified and recognized by the Guinness Book of World Records, making him the individual with the most wishes granted through Make-a-Wish. Cena, despite his fame and fortune, has always made a point of putting charity first and promoting generosity in his fans.

"I can't say enough how cool it is to see the kids so happy, and their families so happy, I truly want to show them that it's their day...I just drop everything. I don't care what I'm doing,"

Cena has made sure that the focus is always on the time that he contributes, rather than any financial donation to charities. Time is something we cannot get back and so it becomes the most precious thing to donate. Behind the huge, behemoth of a man who throws people around inside the ring is a very kind-hearted soul who still receives, and attends to, dozens of *Make-a-Wishes* every year.

ON TRACK TO A BRIGHTER FUTURE

Seemingly, it's very difficult to do anything in this world without inexorably destroying it. We know now, in the 2020s, that the effects of the last 200 years of industrial and technological growth have harmed the planet, and will continue to do so. Climate groups have risen in every nation across Earth, schoolchildren have protested in several countries in recent years, and demands are being heard from the population to *do something to stop it*.

Let's be clear: the threats of climate change are severe and could lead to widespread famine, poverty, and death. Climate change is one of the most commonly reported news stories, and its relevancy grows year after year as new studies are carried out.

The good news is that people *are* doing something to help fight it. Scientists, inventors, and generally, boffins the world over are working tirelessly to revolutionize how the world works. Ultimately, our travel, food, and consumer goods need to change so that they're more sustainable. The United Kingdom has been producing massive amounts of energy from wind, which is beginning to be exported to Europe. Norway currently profits from hydropower, selling it to countries for a cheaper price than coal and oil. Companies in America have begun the mammoth task of reducing ocean waste, starting with the Great Pacific Garbage Patch.

A real positive comes from Germany, which launched the world's first trains to run on hydrogen in 2022. Hydrogen is a reliable source of fuel and Alstom developed the technology, and it is said that it is also remarkably efficient. The train produces steam and condensed water as byproducts, both of which don't negatively affect the environment, and one tank will power the train for over 600 miles. It's a good start to replacing the 4,000 diesel-powered trains in Germany alone.

There's a long way to go but get behind the projects that work toward a happier future for the world's youth. They'll thank you if you do.

THEY'RE REALLY JUST THAT POLITE, EH?

Quick, think of three stereotypes about Canadians…

If you didn't say maple syrup, snow, and being polite, then you're a liar. Canada is a wonderful country that has all the extremes of geography and weather that a person could want, as well as a litany of dangerous wildlife if an Australian is feeling homesick. In most of the country, Canadians observe a lovely holiday known as Family Day in February of every year, a long weekend that one may very well spend with your family. But it also allows many stores to close so workers can enjoy some time off. That's what Food Basics, a store in Kingston, Ontario, intended to do in 2019.

However, for a reason that is yet to have been deciphered, on that Family Day, the doors to the store were left open. Of course, there were no workers that day as they were all off enjoying whatever they were doing, and customers soon began to turn up.

Take a brief moment to think about how citizens in your hometown would react to a grocery store whose doors were open, yet no soul was in the shop. It would be safe to say that in many cities, towns, and villages, there would be a decent chunk of the population who would take the opportunity to steal a few items while there was no one to tell them off. If you follow the logic through, it wouldn't be that far-fetched to imagine looting if it got really out of hand.

In Kingston, the situation thankfully didn't go that way. An eyewitness reported standing outside the store, considering whether he should go inside as he couldn't *really* purchase anything. He then spied a man walking out the front of the store holding two packages of tomatoes and the eyewitness called to him:

"Hey, buddy! You just taking some tomatoes?"

"I left $5 on the counter."

It's worth pointing out that $5 was overpaying for the tomatoes, even after tax is taken into account. Police officers arrived at the store by about 4:30 p.m. and informed the store owner that the shop was open. The owner spooled through the surveillance footage and found no evidence that anyone had stolen anything. People had paid for the produce they took, and no crime was committed. Where else other than Canada could you leave a store open all day, unattended, and still receive money for the produce? (Don't tell your boss - otherwise, they'll realize they don't actually need you to make a profit!)

IN CE LAB RAT ION
OF YOUR CONTRIBUTION!

Humans have a lot to owe to mice. Not everyone's a fan of them, but they have (unwillingly) played an important role in scientific research for the last century. Mice share a few similarities with people. Mice age, they are mammals, their hormones are similar, they are 80% genetically identical, and they also loved the musical *Hamilton*.

The use of mice and rats has led to many important discoveries such as treatment for acute leukemia, vaccinations for both polio and meningitis, and development of a treatment for breast cancer. All in all, their contribution is invaluable to the human race and who knows what more is to come. In the 2020s, encouraging signs of slowing progression of dementia have been seen in laboratory mice as well as further medications to help fight cancer. Who knows what more we will owe to the little furry creatures?

To recognize this, in 2013, a sculpture was cast in bronze for a monument to the humble laboratory mouse to be placed outside the Institute of Cytology and Genetics in Russia. The sculpture features a cartoon mouse, sitting atop a pedestal. The mouse holds knitting needles in its paws and knits a double helix strand of DNA. The DNA spiral winds to the left, showing how much work there is yet to be done as the strand is incomplete and not fully understood, but it also shows how far humans and mice have come.

The scientific community has hailed the monument as a wonderful step toward recognizing a silent voice in the catalog of scientific discovery. The sculptor Andrei Kharkevich describes the statue as showing the scientist and mouse "interconnected," demonstrating that they serve the same purpose together.

While we'd all agree that the fewer animals used for the progression of science, the better, it's humbling to see some sort of tribute made to those who already have been.

MORGAN BEEMAN

Throughout the 2010s and 2020s, people learned a great deal about bees and their impact on life on Earth. Most of us have learned in our early years of education that bees pollinate flowers and make honey, but people are being educated further about what bees actually *do*. Bees, potentially, are what makes the natural world work. Bees pollinate far more than flowers; it is estimated honeybees pollinate approximately one-third of the food that makes it to our plates. A study claims that if the bees disappeared, then some $5.7bn would be lost from the global economy due to the enormous hit on vegetation and crop yield.

Unfortunately, the bee population has been shrinking for a while now due to pesticides, parasites, and loss of habitat, all of which humans can help with, and many are trying - such as actor Morgan Freeman.

Freeman is one of Hollywood's most prolific and recognized actors, appearing in movies such as *The Shawshank Redemption, The Dark Knight*, and *Seven*, just to name three out of a very, very long list. Since 2014, Freeman has been indulging in a new hobby, bee-keeping. In fact, the actor owns a 124-acre ranch and is committed to turning it into a bee *sanctuary*. Freeman cites the need to keep bees healthy and to keep the population levels high to have a healthy planet as his main motivation.

For a reason that eludes most sensible people, Freeman doesn't wear any protective gear when bee-keeping. He refuses to take honey from them, so claims that he's no threat to the bees. He simply wanders up to their hives to observe them or provide some food and, presumably because of his honorable intentions, they have never stung him.

Not all of us have more than 100 acres of land that we can transform into a sanctuary for animals, but we can do our little bit by being kind to the bugs of the world. They contribute a lot more than we give them credit for. Plus, if we're really mean and they rise up to fight us, then we *will* lose. Do not tell them, though. The last thing humans need is a big bug revolution!

NO SMALLS' FEAT

The Transatlantic Slave Trade will go down in history as one of humanity's greatest tragedies. For approximately a quarter of a millennium, it robbed millions of people of their basic humanity in the name of profiteering and cruelty. European countries such as Britain, Spain, France, and Portugal began abolishing slavery in the early 19th century, and the movement of abolition spread into America. America's economy, for approximately a century, was dependent on the goods produced from slavery. Many were reluctant to bring an end to a process that brought such wealth to the country. In essence, the disagreement over whether to abolish slavery or not was the primary cause of the American Civil War. It was only with the Northern States' victory that the ghastly trade was abolished in 1865.

Life for Black people in America wasn't exactly easy after the abolition. Their freedom had been constitutionally secured, but racist attitudes prevailed, and it took a further century for their full rights to be guaranteed. However, things had drastically improved for Black people and few exemplify this change in status better than Robert Smalls.

Smalls was born into slavery in 1839 and worked for the first third of his life in servitude to his master. He witnessed vile mistreatment of Black people. When the American Civil War broke out in 1861, Smalls was employed by the Confederate (slavery-supporting) Army to steer the ship *CSS Planter*. Smalls did so but was concocting an escape plan with several other enslaved people aboard the ship. In 1862, they stole the *CSS Planter* with the other enslaved workers aboard and their families. They escaped Confederate waters and sailed toward the Union naval fleet, brandishing a white sheet. They had earned their freedom by escaping the Confederacy and shared a large amount of money given to them by the Union states for stealing a boat.

For many, this story would be the incredible apex of their life - it sounds like something you'd witness in a movie. However, Smalls' story doesn't end there. In 1868, after the abolition, he was elected to the South Carolina House of Representatives. There, he worked hard to introduce free compulsory schooling for children in South Carolina, before introducing the Civil Rights Bill that granted access to public services for all citizens.

Smalls gained election to the United States House of Representatives in 1874 and fought for the safety of Black Americans in the Southern States. Smalls is honored today in several ways, with a ship, fort, and part of a highway having been named after him. He showed immense strength in reversing his fortunes from being enslaved to being a leader and protectorate of Black people when their rights were actively being attacked by other politicians.

YOU CAN'T ASK FOR MUCH
MOORE THAN THAT, TOM

Do you remember the COVID-19 pandemic? Of course, you do. Unless you're a *very* young child, then you'll recall the years of disruption to normal life and general fear around the world when the disease emerged in 2019. Depending on what country you're from/or were in during 2020 (the year of the first major lockdowns) then your interpretation of the whole affair will be different. Some countries locked down pretty much instantly such as New Zealand and managed to contain their initial outbreak. Other countries such as Italy and the United States struggled with managing their cases and suffered high infection and death rates.

One country that similarly had a difficult time was the United Kingdom. The UK took a long time, compared with other European countries, to enforce a lockdown. The country could have done without the economic hit, and British people tend to grumble when they've been told what to do. When the UK announced that they were locking down in March 2020, the mood was bleak in the country. Deaths continued to soar and the months rumbled on.

If you ask someone from the UK about notable events from the pandemic, then they'll likely mention scotch eggs, half-price meals at restaurants, and Captain Tom Moore. Moore was a retired British Army officer who approached his 100th birthday during the pandemic. He made headlines when he decided to raise money for the NHS, the UK's National Health Service, which was working exceptionally hard to contain outbreaks of coronavirus. Tom aimed to earn £1,000 (US $1,285) by the time he turned 100 by walking the length of his garden and back to his house as many times as he felt he could. In the end, Tom raised £32.9m (US $42.3m).

Tom received 150,000 birthday cards on his 100th birthday and was honored in many ways, including being knighted by the then monarch, Queen Elizabeth II. His story helped give a little boost to many people who were suffering through the pandemic with loneliness and sickness. Watching a 100-year-old man do his bit for the struggling health service was inspiring and remains one of the enduring images of the pandemic for the people of the United Kingdom.

Tom died in 2021 from pneumonia while testing positive for coronavirus. He died a national hero.

HOW TO SECURE
YOUR REPUTATION

The monarchy is a tough subject to bring up in Britain. Not everyone thinks it's a good thing to have in the 21st century, while some people believe it's a great symbol of national pride. But you'll start a debate by mentioning it in a pub. Consider yourself double-dared to do so if you're ever in London; triple points if you bring it up somewhere trendy like Islington or Tottenham. This debate (argument, really) is what highlights the peculiarity of the almost universally liked character that is Princess Diana.

Princess Diana was the wife of Prince Charles (Now King Charles III) from 1981 to 1992, and during the marriage, Diana earned a glowing reputation among the UK population. Most notably, Diana gave a lot of her time to charity, raising awareness for many worthy causes outside of traditional Royal engagements. She became President of Barnardo's, a children's charity, as well as acting as patron of the Natural History Museum. All in all, Diana represented over a hundred charities during her time as Princess and continued her work after her divorce from Charles in 1996.

Her most significant contribution, which partly led to her hero status within the LGBTQ+ community, came in the 1980s when she began her work with HIV/AIDS patients. It's important to recognize that, in the 1980s, there was a huge amount of fear associated with HIV/AIDS. The disease is exceptionally serious and even now, in the 21st century, there is no absolute cure, and it remains a remarkably difficult condition to live with. When it emerged in the 1980s, particularly among homosexual male communities, the diagnosis came with an awareness that death would follow shortly after. Understanding was poor and TV adverts warning the public about the disease only ingrained some misconceptions further.

Today we know that HIV/AIDS is passed on only through intimate bodily contact. In the early stages of awareness, this wasn't known by most people. Diana engaged with the research behind HIV/AIDS and held a great deal of sympathy for those who had the disease. In 1987, she visited a ward with AIDS patients in it, who would likely die soon from the illness, and held hands with one of the patients. The photograph of Diana shaking hands with the man, without gloves or form of protective equipment, was of extreme significance. The photograph challenged commonly held views and showed that one could be near AIDS patients and interact normally with them without being at risk. That singular moment, along with Diana's constant and public charity work with HIV/AIDS patients, helped de-stigmatize the illness for many people and move awareness away from disgust and more toward empathy.

"HIV does not make people dangerous to know. You can shake their hands and hug them. Heaven knows they need it. What's more, you can share their homes, their workplaces, and their playgrounds and toys."

CHANGING MILLIONS OF LIVES IS WORTH FAR MORE THAN BILLIONS

If there's anything to be learned from medical advancement in the 20th century, it's that it's a moneymaker. The health sector makes a vast amount of money for industry leaders and company directors because they offer something that is very often unavailable anywhere else. Until recently, in the US, insulin (a common and necessary drug for diabetic patients) could regularly cost $300. In February 2023, Eli Lilly (a company that manufactures insulin) announced that they would cut the cost for customers to $35, which still means that the company makes back more than three times what it spends to make it - and were heavily praised for their generosity.

The health industry making profits is something that many people struggle to come to terms with. Many countries across the world have access to universally available healthcare, such as the United Kingdom, Canada, Germany, and Japan. The citizens of these countries have access to life-saving healthcare for no payment beyond their tax money and a standardized cost for prescription medication. For these citizens, pharmaceutical development is not generally seen as a money-maker, but the scientists and companies who make the medication stand to make an inordinate amount of money by making the drug *first*.

In 1955, a man called Jonas Salk stood on the precipice of being a multi-millionaire, if not a billionaire, for creating an effective polio vaccine. He decided to turn down that opportunity.

After World War II, Salk was a young and ambitious scientist with serious promise. The institution gave him a lab of his own at the University of Pittsburgh School of Medicine where he decided to devote his life to finding a vaccine for polio. Salk spent the first year gathering researchers and other scientists to join his team, and he started experimenting. Another scientist by the name of Albert Sabin was working on an oral vaccine using strains of the disease that were alive, something that Salk saw as being dangerous and leading to failure. He decided that using a dead strain would be safer and yield good results.

The funding poured in for Salk because the world was terrified of polio and support for a cure was high. It's important to remember that polio was a deadly illness that had high incidence numbers. In 1952, 21,000 people were paralyzed due to the disease in America alone. The popular United States president Franklin D Roosevelt fell to the disease in 1945, which also framed the desire for eradication. In all, by 1955, $67m had been donated to Salk's project.

Salk began testing his vaccine on children, and by 1954, almost one million children formed the polio pioneers who were part of a wave of mass testing to ensure that the vaccine would work across a large selection of people. It proved successful, and the vaccine was announced as safe in 1955. Salk decided not to patent his vaccine which has gone on to save millions of people's lives. Polio rates plummeted worldwide after 1955. When asked on TV who owns the patent to his lifesaving work, he responded thusly:

"Well, the people I would say. There is no patent. Could you patent the sun?"

The value of a patent for Salk's polio vaccine, if it existed, sits at approximately $7bn.

EINSTEIN VS. RACISM

Albert Einstein probably goes down as the most well-recognized scientist of all time, with the image of his smiling face and tongue sticking out toward the camera being synonymous with his name. Einstein was a German physicist who migrated to the United States years before the outbreak of World War II due to his opposition to Adolf Hitler's politics. His discoveries in the early 20th century helped shape modern physics and laid a foundation for several hundreds of physicists to advance his work.

Einstein was glad to leave Germany when he did, having observed his country fall to the Nazis under coercion and manipulation. He helped America by informing on German war plans, especially the nuclear weapons program under development in Germany - he advised the Allies to do the same. Yet Einstein found some aspects of life difficult in America and was outspoken about the ongoing mistreatment of Black Americans.

Until the mid-1960s, America didn't legally see Black Americans as having the same worth or social standing as White Americans. This led to segregated schools, buses, parks, and public facilities, which Einstein publicly abhorred. He had been subject to anti-

Semitism in Germany before he left for America and, following World War II, he felt that the world had seen the effect that racism could have on a country if left unchecked.

In 1946, Einstein visited Lincoln University, a historically Black university, to lecture students about physics. The American media largely ignored the color photo of Einstein lecturing in front of a small congregation of pupils in suits, in all likelihood because of the comment made by Einstein concerning the visit:

> *"My trip to this institution was on behalf of a worthwhile cause...There is a separation of colored people from white people in the United States. That separation is not a disease of colored people. It's a disease of white people."*

Many American media outlets wouldn't have been brave enough in the late 1940s to criticize openly the racist politics of the time, even if they were just quoting Einstein himself. The visit to Lincoln University was one of very few for Einstein at this time, as his health had been declining for some time. He chose Lincoln University as the exception to provide some form of publicity for the university and to ensure that he was contributing something to providing social justice for Black Americans.

THE MOTHER OF ALL
WORKERS OF AMERICA

Unions.

A word that, for some, causes an instant swelling of vomit in the back of the throat while for others, it's a source of pride. If you're a worker, then unions are there for you; they're supposed to help workers procure better pay and working conditions, and sometimes simply to make sure that workers are being treated like human beings.

Someone who fought hard for workers' rights at the end of the 19th century, managing to increase the membership of the United Mine Workers of America from 10,000 to 300,000, was the woman who became known as "Mother Jones." That's a feat that would be impressive in most online communities of the 21st century, let alone in a turn-of-the-century group of workers. She was dubbed the "most dangerous woman in America" in 1902 and self-described herself as "a hell-raiser". How did one (supposedly elderly) woman manage to become so influential at a time when women weren't afforded basic democratic rights such as voting rights and ownership of property?

Mother Jones (Mary G. Harris Jones) was born in 1837 in Ireland. Mary had four children by the age of 30 and a happy married life, but she lost all her children due to a horrific outbreak of yellow fever. When her husband died, she lost everything else, as her identity was legally wrapped up with him. The home was owned by him, Mary had no job beyond housekeeping, and her identity was "wife." Mary decided to emigrate to Chicago to work as a dressmaker, a business that she lost in 1871 to a fire.

Mary disappeared from the historical record for approximately 20 years at this point. She lived among the working class of America, seeing their plight, poor living conditions, and low wages compared with the richer echelons of society. By the turn of the century, Mary had developed a persona as a witty, angry, elderly, public speaker. In the early 1900s, women were to be meek and quiet, but Mary wouldn't adhere to this. She was angry about the marginalized working classes and the greedy business owners who exploited them. She wore large, antique dresses that aged her and adopted the name of Mother Jones, as she was seen as the mother to all workers.

Mother Jones organized strikes against corrupt mine owners, was falsely imprisoned, and encouraged child miners to fight against their cruel employment. Jones lives on through her words, still echoed by unions to this day:

"Pray for the dead and fight like hell for the living."

She holds a place in the National Women's Hall of Fame and is seen as a hero by the miners still. Her work helped unify those with little at a time when women were expected to accept their place in society and not speak up. She would have been very proud to have been called the "most dangerous woman in America."

"LET'S AGREE NEVER TO DO THAT AGAIN"

There's a chance that you have not heard of Liechtenstein before. If you *have* heard of it, then there's an even greater chance that you couldn't tell anyone anything about the place. Liechtenstein is a very small country (sixth-smallest worldwide) that sits between Austria and Switzerland and has a tiny population of less than 40,000. The area became known as the country of Liechtenstein in the early 18th century, though spent years with a close relationship to Germany.

Liechtenstein does not have much interest in conflict, probably given its tiny size (only 62 square miles). It would make no sense for the small country to involve itself in wars that it would likely lose. During the Austro-Prussian war of 1866, Liechtenstein men made themselves available to the Empire of Austria, mainly to ensure that the area of Tyrol would remain safe. Liechtenstein went on to pledge an almighty force of 80 soldiers to the conflict, which saw the death of 170,000 soldiers in total.

Liechtenstein's story in the conflict has achieved an almost legendary status amongst historians, for if you boil it down, it's hilarious and almost adorable. Liechtenstein sent 80 soldiers off to war, a force of 81 soldiers returned, and then Liechtenstein disbanded its military.

The story is, in principle, true. Legend says that the extra soldier was an opposition solider who defected to the small nation. Instead, it seems more likely that it was an Austrian liaison officer on the same side who joined, not an opponent. Regardless, after the war ended and the German Confederation dissolved shortly afterwards, Liechtenstein dissolved its small military force and announced its permanent neutrality.

Liechtenstein has not become involved in any military action since 1866, unbelievably managing to retain its neutrality during the world wars of the 20th century. During World War II, when the Nazis marched into Austria, the prince of Liechtenstein went to Berlin to visit Adolf Hitler and guaranteed the nation's safety, somehow.

Liechtenstein remains a neutral country to this day, with an inactive military. It's worth visiting to see how an incredibly peaceful nation operates from its small valley in the Alps.

Ain't No Mountain High Enough!

You know when you're faced with a task to do, either at work or in your own home, and you put it off for so long that eventually, it seems as if there's no point doing it because is there *really* a need anymore? Well, this particular urge doesn't seem to have occurred to Dashrath Manjhi, an Indian man from the poor village of Gehlaur, born in 1934.

Manjhi had never been a man of very much fortune, either in the sense of good luck or monetarily. He'd left the village to earn some money mining when he was young before returning to his home and marrying. Gehlaur is situated on a plain that is bordered by a steep mountain made from quartzite, preventing simple access to a bigger nearby town. The mountain has long been a problem for the people, lengthening journeys to a point far beyond inconvenient. It's also dangerous, as Manjhi found out in 1959 when his wife Falguni Devi fell from the mountain and died from her injuries.

Many blamed the mountain for Falguni Devi's death as the mountain delayed gaining access to doctors or any decent medical services. Manjhi certainly did and vowed to do something about it. Manjhi told the villagers that he was going to cut a roadway into the mountain that would render the village more accessible. He was laughed out of town - luckily, not literally. He said that he felt a yearning to contribute more to society, especially to the small community that he loved and began his work in 1960.

Majhi spent 22 years completing the job. In that time, he carved a 360-foot-long path, 23 feet deep and 30 feet wide at points, which formed a functional, working road that reduced the journey to the town drastically. It wasn't only his village; some 60 additional villages gained easier access to healthcare and work that was only a few kilometers away.

Majhi's work is inspiring. He's a man who literally carved through a mountain one shovelful at a time to make life easier for other people, increasing connectivity even when he had his doubters. Though it certainly didn't stay that way…

"Though most villagers taunted me at first, there were quite a few who lent me support later by giving me food and helping me buy my tools."

Somewhere in this story, there's a lesson about perseverance and not giving up when times are difficult, see if you can find it. If you do, tweet about it.

USING SUNLIGHT
TO PAY THE STAFF

Balancing budgets in public facilities is a never-ending, thankless task. Hospitals, police stations, postal services, and other public services are seemingly always without decent financial support. This is doubly true for schools.

Schools provide a service that is completely necessary for most societies to function: free education for all unless they can arrange alternative provisions for themselves. The problem with the entire system is that it largely doesn't function properly. Schools are forever in debt and making cuts to their budget. Teachers remain overworked and underpaid in most countries, there aren't enough teaching assistants, expensive energy bills cause cutbacks on things like trips, and the bottom line is that when there's not enough education money, the children suffer.

So how does one balance the books? For Batesville High School in Batesville, Arkansas, the solution presented itself when an energy company conducted an audit of the Batesville school district. The audit revealed that the district spent an astonishing $600,000 on utility bills annually, leaving the district with so few funds that teachers were leaving due to budget constraints. Despite this relatively doom-laden report, the auditor did a bit of calculating and worked out that the entire district could *save* $2.4m over 20 years if the high school was fitted out with solar panels and all schools received updated lighting, heating, and windows.

The superintendent, Michael Hester, saw the potential immediately and the game-changing energy program sprang into life. Within three years, the energy consumption of the entire district dropped so much that the existing $250,000 deficit transformed into a $1.8m surplus. Hester decided that the first port of call was to bump up all educators' salaries from $2–3,000 across the board to entice them into staying. The district is wealthier and has some exemplary teacher retention levels, often an indicator of a system's success and consistent education.

Across America, other schools have been following suit and have only brought benefits to the pupils they teach. Solar power is raising teachers' salaries, freeing up money for better resources, and helping to reduce the impact on the planet.

A REAL-LIFE,
11-YEAR-OLD, SUPERHERO

What does it mean to be heroic? If you go to Wikipedia and look up "hero" then the opening definition reads thus:

"A hero is a real person or a main fictional character who, in the face of danger, combats adversity through feats of ingenuity, courage, or strength."

In this sense, how often do people get the chance to be heroes? To be presented with an opportunity to be brave or courageous? More worryingly, how many times do we pass up the chance to be a hero? You may be thinking to yourself, "Well, I have been a hero on many occasions." If so, congratulations. Perhaps you've had moments of standing up to a bully, preventing someone from facing violence, putting out a fire, or rescuing a drowning puppy. If you've done any of these things, chances are that you now have a story that you can tell forever, routinely trotting it out at dinner parties accompanied by a meek smile and an "Okay, okay, do you really want to hear it?"

What if you accomplished two heroic acts, that saved people's lives, in one day…, all before your 12th birthday?

On December 9, 2021, Davyon Johnson went to school on what may have felt like a completely normal day. Davyon wanted to become an EMT (Emergency Medical Technician) and was working hard at school, and out of it, to achieve that dream job. On this particular day, a peer accidentally swallowed the cap of his water bottle when trying to drink from it. The pupil's airway closed off, and he stumbled around the corridor and then into Davyon's classroom, desperate for help. Davyon sprang to action, jumping out of his chair and quickly performing the Heimlich Maneuver with all the strength he could muster. The bottle cap popped out of the boy's mouth, and Davyon was cheered and celebrated by his classmates who couldn't believe they'd just seen him save someone's life.

For many of us, this is about as good as a "normal" day at school can get. But that wasn't the end of Davyon's heroism. He set off for home that evening, ready proudly to tell his mother what he'd done - but on the way, he spied a house on fire! The 11-year-old boy noticed a disabled woman attempting to escape the burning house, and he ran across the road to escort her out of the burning building. He says he was just being "a good citizen."

Davyon Johnson was awarded a certificate naming him an honorary deputy for the Sheriff's office in Muskogee, Oklahoma later that month along with some glowing words from his principal. Davyon had learned how to perform the Heimlich Maneuver by watching YouTube. It just goes to show that not everything's useless on there.

SAVING THE EARTH TEN BILLION TREES AT A TIME

We have known for several decades that deforestation on Earth is out of control. Deforestation is the act of clearing forests by cutting down trees and burning shrubbery, something that several industries have relied upon. Trees are useful for an innumerable number of reasons, and it's highly unlikely that humans are going to stop chopping them down any time soon, but we do need to slow down drastically.

The Amazon Rainforest has lost 17% of its forest due to deforestation, something climate scientists have called catastrophic, while the world loses 6m hectares of forest every year, about half the size of Portugal. The forests are crucial to combatting CO_2 levels as the plants and trees in forests help, through photosynthesis, to take CO_2 out of the atmosphere and provide higher levels of oxygen (which we need to live, obviously!). The United Nations is aware of the dangers of deforestation and many countries are now committed to The Bonn Challenge, which started in 2020 and is due to finish in 2030. The challenge is to restore 150m hectares of deforested land in ten years.

The challenge has been met with great enthusiasm in many rural areas across the planet. It brings massive amounts of work and funding to areas that desperately need it. And that's not to speak of the benefits that rural communities gain from having a developing forest nearby. A total of 28 African countries have made a pledge that reaches approximately 113 million hectares, with Ethiopia planting four billion trees in 2019 alone.

Pakistan has committed itself to the cause more so than most. They drew headlines in 2014 by pledging themselves to their Billion Tree Tsunami. The tsunami will take Pakistan past its commitment to the Bonn Challenge. It will restore 350,000 hectares of forests and take approximately ten billion trees to fulfill. The United Nations Environment Programme complimented Pakistan's contribution to fighting for the good of the planet and hailed it as an example for all countries that are looking to reforest:

"We are at a point in history where we need to act and Pakistan is leading on this important effort."

It's encouraging to know that world leaders are putting an effort into re-forestation, which should help tackle the massive damage currently being done to our planet. If you're looking to go traveling, or are young without much of an idea of what you want to "do" with your life, going to help plant trees is not only a helpful thing you could do, but you get paid an okay amount to do it. Plus, you get to spend your day listening to music as you exist in a natural environment somewhere gorgeous - while saving the planet!

STANDING UP TO GREED

Utah Lake has been the site of a grizzly legal battle during the 2020s. The lake is a large body of water that has had its fair share of pollution problems, with efforts being made to counter these in the last few years. It sits as an important migratory spot for birds; millions flock to nest on its shore each year to feed on the further millions of fish that live within it. The ecosystem is recovering from pollution thanks to the work of scientists and ecologists such as Ben Abbot, a professor at Brigham Young University who fought to protect the lake from developers and won.

In 2018, a Dubai-backed investment group called Lake Restoration Solutions (LRS), made their plans for the development of the lake public, to the shock of researchers. LRS had plans to dredge the lake, removing massive amounts of water, vegetation, and habitats to create artificial islands. LRS claims that the islands would create greater passages through the lake as well as helping to tackle Lake Utah's pollution problem. Of course, the plan came with designs to build properties on those islands that would be sold off to private owners at a premium.

Enter stage left, Ben Abbot. Abbot openly opposed the plans, publishing a series of articles and statements about what he considered "shady" operations from the company, as well as a lack of scientific basis in their plans. LRS responded by suing him for defamation and brought him to court at the beginning of 2023. If LRS had managed to prove that Abbot's words were designed to bring unfair disrepute to the company, then they could have proceeded with the project that had already been OK'd by several members of the local government.

The judge ruled that Abbot hadn't said anything incorrect. In fact, bar the word "shady," the judge found that nothing said had come close to defamation and that his claims were simply accurate points about the project. The defamation lawsuit was thrown out of court and LRS was ordered to pay all legal fees associated. Abbot has gone on to counter-sue the company over their attempts to defame him by destroying his reputation and the attempted development of Utah Lake has been abandoned.

Too often has greed won in our world, and it's emboldening to watch someone fight against that, to stand up and demand a stop to the destruction of our natural world for extra profit.

LOANING AN ARGUMENT

How often do you get the chance to talk to someone you don't know about anything at all? Perhaps a debate on politics or a discussion on something in your personal life that's on your mind. Maybe you'd like the chance to be able to listen, rather than to be the one talking for once.

Especially in our post-COVID world, people's ability to strike up conversations with another person has been greatly diminished. It's so easy to look at your phone, chatting virtually with a friend who could be hundreds of miles away, rather than attempt to engage with someone who's in the same café as you. The truth is it's difficult to do this. To just turn round to someone and say, "Hello, I'm alone today, would you like to talk about things while we drink our coffee?" It may be misconstrued as an attempted flirt or, worse, that you're not well and should be committed to the nearest Asylum for the Perpetually Outgoing. But in essence, this is the very notion that the Human Library is built on.

The Human Library is an initiative that started in Denmark in 2000. The idea is that you get the chance to talk to people you wouldn't normally talk to. This may mean a conservative individual talks to a more liberal person, politically, and has a reasoned discussion to understand each other's points of view. A younger person may have the chance to discuss the generational divide with someone older. Perhaps a comfortable, middle-class person who doesn't understand the effects of poverty and privilege in society gets the chance to discuss that with someone from a lower economic background.

In essence, it's about getting us all talking and has been hailed as a great combater of loneliness and for promoting reasoned discussion when it is desperately needed. The Human Library operates in such a way that it lends out people (volunteers) rather than books. The library borrower then sits with their loaned individual and talks. The people in the library are volunteers who believe in the nature of the project. Politeness is key in the discourse. The Human Library has gone from strength to strength as the years have passed by, with more libraries joining across the world. Many human libraries are one-off events, but there may be a full-time, physical library not far away from you.

GIVING A LITTLE BACK

Can you imagine actually being a billionaire? Having more money to your name than 99.9% of people who'll ever live and more than some countries? We've all had dreams of gaining vastly more money than we have and need. We've thought of the frivolous expenditure on things we don't need, such as a new car or holiday properties all over the world, and we've also all thought about the good that we might do with the money. Whether it's tackling world hunger or helping to solve the homelessness crisis, being amazingly wealthy provides so many opportunities that it can be a surprise that so many uber-wealthy people don't take those chances - not just for good, but also for bad!

As such, it's pleasant when we see a billionaire take the opportunity to do something good for the world. In 2022, Mark Cuban launched the Cost Plus Drugs website and company and has potentially unveiled a route for millions of North Americans to access life-saving medication without becoming bankrupt in the process.

If you're not American, chances are you know about its healthcare system. The system is private, meaning that ultimately the cost of treatment and medication comes back to the patient and their insurers. This is instead of a public health system such as European countries have. This can mean that some patients pay a large amount of money to afford medication to help them combat illness, something that Cost Plus Drugs aims towards to help people.

Cuban is a billionaire who made his money through his investments in entertainment channels especially due to his sale of Broadcast.com, which he sold to Yahoo for $5.7bn in 1999. Cuban says that he was emailed in 2018 by radiologist Alexander Oshmyansky, who pitched an idea for a business to him. The business would be based on manufacturing generic drugs, unattached to brands or wholesalers, which meant that all of the money spent would go to the manufacturer and all savings would be passed onto the consumer.

The upshot when Cost Plus Drugs was launched, was that the retailers, who are typically responsible for the markup on prescription meds, were avoided. The customers directly pay for medication without the involvement of insurance companies and the savings are astronomical.

If you visit the website, you can see what sort of savings we're talking about and why this service is crucial for so many Americans. Available cancer medications range from $60–$3,000 cheaper than at retail, making life-saving treatment a far more viable option for people suffering from the world's most common terminal disease.

This story unfortunately requires a system to exist that puts a burden on sick people in the first place. But the fact that a billionaire has chosen to invest his capital in an enterprise that will, in all likelihood, bring very little financial gain is something that should be celebrated and encouraged.

ALMOST THE SAME, JUST CHEAPER, BETTER AND NICER FOR EVERYONE

The trade of animal products such as ivory and rhino horns ranks as one of the world's most damaging enterprises and seemingly remains out of control. People have sought animal products such as ivory for thousands of years. Humans have traditionally enjoyed how ivory looks and how it can be fashioned into jewelry or decorative pieces. Many societies value its use as medicine.

Illegal poaching of Rhino horn over the centuries has caused irreversible damage. Rhinos have been alive for at least 40 million years, yet after all this time, three out of five species of rhino are critically endangered. The drastic drop in the numbers of rhinos is entirely down to human activity, and poachers continue to attack the endangered animals, only concerned with their own profit. In countries such as Vietnam and China, the horn is mistakenly believed to help cure numerous health problems such as cancer. A single horn is worth $100,000 in the market, which is currently valued at $500m.

The situation Is not great, but the countries where rhinos live naturally, in Africa and Asia, are putting more money into their protection. Poachers are less successful than they used to be and face death if they attempt to hunt rhinos. A promising product has emerged from California that may help to reduce the need for rhino horns in communities in Asia.

Pembient is now able to produce a synthetic product, using proteins that mimic the properties of rhino horn. The company hopes that, over the next few years, they'll be able to capture a quarter of the globe's market for rhino horn, with breweries in Beijing looking to use the "horn" in products they can sell to customers. The synthetic, fake horn will have no ethical or legal problems attached to it, so any trade will not have to be conducted in shady deals. Instead, the product can be purchased from shop shelves. If the demand is drastically cut by the use of clever synthetic products, then poachers will have less motivation to hunt the endangered species, and conservationist efforts can be more fruitful in saving the chubby unicorns.

METAL MUSIC IS
GOOD FOR THE SOUL

You know, metal music fans are so often some of the loveliest and gentlest people on the planet. There's yet to be any significant scientific research into why this is; on the face of it, it seems unlikely if you judge their tattoos, piercings, dyed hair, and abrasive music. But without fail, metal music concerts are accepting spaces where anyone is permitted to attend, audiences are supportive, and smaller bands are given chances to be loved without attracting a vast crowd.

Richard McDeid is a father who discovered the immense, calming effect of the subgenre when his son Mason was crying uncontrollably. Mason has suffered from cerebral palsy since birth and one of his symptoms is being afflicted with crying fits that can take time to come out of. One day, Richard decided to put on Metallica's *Binge and Purge* tape, went to wash the dishes for a few minutes, and then returned to check up on Mason. When he came back, Mason had stopped crying, the first time he had done so without another person helping him.

Without thinking about how he'd done it, Richard had provided Mason with a helpful coping strategy. At first, Mason enjoyed Metallica only, but he branched out to other heavy metal bands as time went by. It quickly became something the father and son could bond over. Since that first time listening to Metallica, Richard and Mason have attended over 1,000 heavy metal concerts. Richard says that they generally get to experience the best that a metalhead could want - front-row action with the world's best (and loudest) artists.

Beyond going to concerts, Richard went a step further in his quest to invest time into Mason's new favorite hobby. He started Mason MetalFest, a benefit concert in Minneapolis for Cerebral Palsy awareness month, with ten local metal bands in attendance. The festival raised money for CP charities and was awarded the Best Show of the Year at the local Metalsota Metty Awards.

Richard has certainly raised the bar for all fathers everywhere, showing exemplary levels of care and devotion to making his son as happy as he could be, in the shadow of a tough illness.

WHAT GOES AROUND, COMES AROUND THREE TIMES OVER

We will all, inevitably, find ourselves facing difficult times in our lives. Unexpected problems will happen and that is just how life is. Still, we lament the extra expenditure that arrives when something expensive needs replacing, especially if that expensive thing is more functional than enjoyment-based. No-one has ever excitedly punched the air as they realize that they're going to have to spend $3,000 on a brand-new boiler.

For Dianne Gordon from Mississippi, in 2022, such an inconvenience struck when her car broke down. Dianne was in no way fortunate enough to be able to afford the necessary fix from the garage, and her insurers wouldn't pay out for a simple breakdown, so she was left without transportation. Dianne started walking two miles to work every day instead and very much got on with her life.

One day, Dianne decided to purchase a snack on the way to work - why not, after all, a four-mile round-walk on top of work leaves with you a calorie deficit. As she walked into a BP gas station, she spied a plastic bag on the floor. She peered inside and saw several wedding invitations and a massive amount of money. Faced with the dilemma, Dianne decided that she wouldn't be able to live with herself if she took the money, particularly if it belonged to people who were looking to be wed soon. Dianne handed it in to the police who were quickly able to track down the couple and reunited them with their funds. All in all, there was $14,780 inside the bag! The couple were exceptionally grateful to Dianne for being so honest and saving their wedding.

For people like Dianne, the thank you is often enough. But a spouse of one of the police officers heard about Dianne's good deed and decided that maybe she required a bit more. A crowdfunding campaign was launched on GoFundMe to raise money for Dianne. In February 2023, with funds raised at $25,000, the campaign worked with a local car dealer to purchase a new car for Dianne.

When the GoFundMe was officially closed, the campaign sat at $82,675 with almost 3,000 people choosing to donate their hard-earned money to Dianne. She bought herself a Jeep!

NOW INTO YEAR EIGHT OF "MEALS WITH STRANGERS"...

If you're American, then Thanksgiving can be an intensely important event. For Americans, spending Christmas with their families isn't quite enough so they celebrate Thanksgiving a month beforehand as well. This ensures that Christmas is full of awkward conversations as nothing new has happened since November. Obviously, that's a joke, but Thanksgiving remains a meaningful time for many Americans and is important for Jamal Hinton and Wanda Dench for a more peculiar reason than most.

In 2016, Jamal, a 17-year-old from Phoenix, received a text message from an unknown number. The text read:

"Thanksgiving at my house, from Grandma"

Jamal frowned and wondered when exactly his grandma had learned how to text, so he asked for a picture of the sender. The sender was Wanda Dench, from Mesa, and this left Jamal a touch confused as to what to do. Wanda seemed nice enough, so he responded:

"Can I still get a plate tho?"

"Of course, you can. That's what grandmas do…, feed everyone."

Slightly bemused, Jamal decided that he would take Wanda up on her offer and arrived at her house for Thanksgiving in November 2016. The Denchs always invited friends for Thanksgiving, so Jamal wasn't the only non-family member there, but he told of how welcoming everyone was. He found the whole thing equally brilliant and hilarious.

Jamal went back in 2017 for Thanksgiving, this time with his girlfriend in tow. He then returned in 2018 and posted a picture on Instagram with the caption - "it's a tradition now." Long story short, the duo has met every year for Thanksgiving and has sparked an unlikely friendship over a strange, accidental text.

At that time, Jamal was there for Wanda after she lost her husband to COVID-19 in 2020. Wanda remarked on *Today* how grateful she was to have met Jamal six years previously. Perhaps there doesn't have to be such a big divide between the generations; it just takes a bit of reaching out and having the nerve to just say "Yes," Wanda said -

"[Jamal] literally changed my life and my point of view on young generations about being open to friendships when you think you have nothing in common with somebody. But when you just sit and talk to them? Oh my gosh.... He's in my heart for life."

ADDICTED TO CHARITY!

A quick note before this story begins: *This book is not an advocate of the lottery. Do not put all your hopes into winning it. Don't think that only good things will come your way if you do!*

That said, here's another lottery story.

Some people are fundamentally giving people. In the UK, the jobs you associate with giving might be positions such as nurses, charity workers, social workers, and teachers, among many others. These people are in a job that requires a lot of work toward a cause that one believes is worth time and effort. Often people in these positions aren't after a great deal of money but receive something from their employment that money can't provide - a sense of happiness and satisfaction that doing their job makes other people's lives better. So, what happens if we *do* give one of these people a massive amount of money?

In 2019, teacher Frances Connelly, along with her husband Patrick, won a princely sum of £115m (US $148m), and their lives changed drastically. Such an enormous amount of money could be used for anything, and some people would surely find a way to burn through it all in a matter of three years with a good enough plan. Frances and Patrick did instantly give money to their friends and family, but then they set up a plan, a yearly charity budget. They would give a certain amount of money away every year while they worked with what they had to ensure that they had more to give later.

The problem is that, by 2022, Frances had managed to donate approximately £60m (US $77m), which took them up to the year 2032 of the plan!

The figure of £60m is an estimate from Frances. She suspects it may be more but has refused to keep a tally in case Patrick finds out exactly how much money has disappeared from their winnings. Frances claims that having the ability to quickly help so many people has become addictive, and she's spent her life, giving things away anyway. She was interviewed in 2022 and asked why she was so happy to see so much money given away. Her response was simple:

"Why not?"

Frances claims that money doesn't really change people; rather, having money liberates you into being who you want to be. So why not take the opportunity to be a generous, loving person? Well said, Frances - and there's no way that the reader of this book would instead take the chance to buy a Bugatti Veyron and a round-the-world cruise that lasted approximately 25 years with that money. Right?

WOMAN WINS
WHAT SHE'S OWED

It's always nice to see someone win when there's been an injustice, especially when that injustice exists because of someone's gender.

In the United Kingdom, what happens to someone's property and finances (their "estate") after they pass away is dictated by the will, an agreement written up by the deceased that explicitly dictates what is to happen. Any arguments with the will can be difficult because the will is that individual's last recorded word about their house, investments, or belongings. Most legal systems will insist on sticking to it. If one doesn't write a will, typically the estate is transferred to the partner if there is one. If not, then the nearest appropriate family member is found and given the estate.

The business of organizing the estate is unpleasant and can lead to arguments between family members over who should receive what and whether the outcome is fair. Often these can be relatively petty disagreements, with many people considering them borderline disrespectful in the wake of a lost life. But how would you feel if, after 66 years of marriage, your partner decided to leave you precisely *nothing* in their will?

This is what faced Harbans Kaur when her husband passed away in 2021. Kaur had six children with her partner Karnail Singh, and she was tasked with raising those children, never working due to her husband's plentiful income, an agreement that the two had. Singh left his entire estate, estimated somewhere between £1.2–1.9m (US $1.5–2.4m), to his two sons, leaving nothing for Kaur to live on beyond her £12,000 (US $15,424) per year state pension.

The ensuing legal battle ended in February 2023, when Harbans Kaur won the entirety of her ex-husband's estate, a potential landmark case for the British legal system. Her lawyer argued that as she was reliant on her husband financially for so many decades while she raised the children, she was not permitted any chance to make her own source of income. To provide her with no help after Singh's death was unfair and to uphold the will as it was would have let down a woman in her early 80s, forcing her into a drastic lifestyle change.

The victory isn't just a victory in this case of a wealthy man being unkind towards his wife. It may mean that vulnerable people are less likely to be left out to dry in similar situations when they need greater help.

Either way, Harbans can now use the money to look after her health, while also sharing it with her six children equally, not just depending on whether or not they're male or female.

IS THE OCEAN
ONE HUGE BATH?

Before you read this story, it's important to know that this book isn't attempting to say that tons of plastic and rubber pouring into the ocean is a good thing, nor a joyous thing. However, if that were to happen, then we'd all hope that it would happen in the most humorous way possible, as it did in 1992.

In 1992, a massive cargo ship heading from China to America faced rough waters and a container broke free from the deck, tumbling into the choppy waters below. Inside were 29,000 ducks. Not real ducks, this isn't *Madagascar*. They were rubber ducks that one might find in their bath or…, someone else's bath. The container opened and 29,000 rubber ducks spilled into the Pacific Ocean, floating atop the gargantuan waves and yard-thick foam.

The scene must have been relatively funny for those on board - until they realized that someone would now be responsible for paying a company that isn't going to receive their 29,000 rubber duckies. The sight of an army of yellow ducks disappearing over every horizon is at least, quite a laugh.

The story doesn't end there. This case was actually studied by scientists, oceanographers, and other related boffins as it was realized that a unique opportunity had been presented. If data was collected accurately as to where the ducks "beached" or "landed," then something could be learned about how the ocean current works across the Pacific Ocean and, potentially, even further than that. American author Donovan Hohn decided he'd produce a piece of work on the strange phenomenon, and he'd do it without leaving his house.

In the end, Hohn's journey took him from Hawaii to Alaska, to the Arctic, and to China as he tracked down the legions of cute yellow ducks. He wrote up the findings and his hilarious journey in the book *Moby-Duck: The True Story of 28,800 Bath Toys Lost at Sea and of the Beachcombers, Oceanographers, Environmentalists and Fools, Including the Author, Who Went in Search of Them.*

The book details the hard work to track down the ducks and remove them from the ocean's ecosystem and the greater awareness gained into the damage of plastic in the ocean. In this way, Hohn helped publicize "garbage patches" that gather in the ocean as plastics, rubbers, and non-perishables gather together, forming a horrific and polluting island of trash. The book highlights the brilliant work of beachcombers and climate scientists who strive to remove the massive amount of plastic damaging the planet.

To this day, ducks are found on beach fronts in the Pacific Ocean (and sometimes the Atlantic Ocean). So, if you find a mysterious yellow rubber duck on the beach one day, there's a good chance it's been in the ocean for more than 30 years.

MAN'S BEST FRIEND,
WITH WINGS

Humans have a strange relationship with animals. Many animals get on with us quite well, such as dogs and cats, while some we merely *wish* got on with us well, such as elephants and tigers, because it would be cool. But our relationship with nature has changed because of our dominance over Earth. Before our city building and resource gathering, we may have been seen very differently in the eyes of the fauna of Planet Earth. Dinner to some, safety to others.

The crow is an animal that in recent decades has gained a reputation for its intelligence, ranking near primates in terms of cognitive ability. Crows show a remarkable knack for problem-solving, managing to use tools to gain access to food and figuring out puzzles that leave many other birds flummoxed. The most curious aspect of the crow remains its relationship with people.

Crows can quite commonly and easily develop a symbiotic relationship with humans, here meaning a mutually beneficial relationship. Tit for tat if you will. In the 19th century, the Vietnamese people (referred to as Annamese at the time) kept crows in a semi-domesticated fashion. Some taught the crows how to speak, even going so far as to use crows to help guard their houses when they were away. The Vietnamese people were quite sure that crows could recognize individual human faces, knowing by sight that one person was a different one than another.

The Vikings also saw something in the crows. The God Odin (God of both War and Death), otherwise known as the All-Father, was depicted in the 7th century accompanied by crows. His crows supposedly possess powers, acting as Odin's eyes and ears in the world, reporting all that may be of interest to the god. This reliance on crows wouldn't be present if the Vikings didn't see intrinsic intelligence in crows; there is clearly a spy-like sneakiness that was interpreted in their manner as well.

We now know that crows get something from humans that encourages their interactions with us. There are many stories of crows bringing shiny objects to humans, some of which they've constructed, in exchange for food. We also know that crows can pass on information about humans they've had contact with and know to be "good" (as it were). Next time you see a crow, maybe throw it a piece of food and see if you can make your dog jealous.

WHAT'S ALL THE
HUB-BLUB HERE THEN?

New Year's Eve celebrations are a big occasion in many cities, towns, and bedrooms across the world. The fireworks and revelry can last well into the morning of the new year, accompanied by the making of mistakes that last well beyond that. So, if you'd been looking forward to your celebrations for the best part of a month (planning your outfits, arrival time, and destination), how would you feel to learn that it has all come crashing down at the last minute? They've canceled the celebrations! You'd probably ask, "Why?" After all, you've spent all of December getting ready for this - how dare they ruin your plans! Then you receive news from your friend's-best friend's cousin, who's married to this guy that, apparently…, there's a walrus.

You read that correctly, the 2022–23 New Year's Eve celebrations in Scarborough, England were canceled after a walrus arrived in the town's harbor!

The walrus in question was an Arctic walrus, a rare sighting in the UK. Thor (that's his name) beached itself in the harbor of Scarborough in late December 2022, and thousands of people desperately clambered to see him. The town became backed up with traffic, people were late to work, and deliveries were delayed as tourists from near and far desperately peered at the giant animal.

The local authorities acted quickly, and the RSPCA (Royal Society for the Prevention of Cruelty to Animals) issued a statement:

> *"Please do not worry -he appears well and is just taking a well-deserved rest after his long adventure!"*

Thor rested at the harbor for several days before making his way further north, but this meant that the town's coveted New Year's fireworks couldn't be lit, as they would certainly stress him out. The townsfolk weren't too concerned with this. Most amused locals were simply grateful to have witnessed such an odd and impressive sight as an Arctic Walrus in their hometown.

Thor moved on after a few days, but he left a note saying he'll be back next year, and he hopes to see "a proper celebration" then.

RAMSAY'S BAD
BOYS BAKERY

Gordon Ramsay, the renowned celebrity chef, is best known for his fiery temper and superb culinary skills. Ramsay, however, has an interest in crime and the impact it can have on someone's future. He has seen firsthand, through family members, what impact drug addiction and crime can have on people. Because of this, he has often engaged himself with charitable causes and with the justice system, to provide individuals with help where he can. In 2012, he took on the unique challenge of helping inmates at Brixton Prison in South London set up a bakery that would teach them cooking skills and provide them with a sense of purpose. The initiative broadcast as *Gordon Behind Bars* helped bring funds to the project in the first place.

The prison kitchen was kitted out with high-quality baking equipment, in order to create products that the public would be willing to spend their money on. Ramsay personally oversaw the training of the inmates, teaching them baking techniques that he had perfected over his years as a Michelin-star chef. The bakery was called Bad Boys Bakery, and it became a hit with the public. They sold the first batch of products through a pop-up shop in Covent Garden in London.

The Ministry of Justice at the time of the broadcast, Kenneth Clarke, was complimentary of the quality of baked goods and of the intent behind the program. He wanted to see similar initiatives rolled out across the country at other prisons, to help provide prisoners with a purpose while they were serving time. However, the bakery provided help beyond preoccupation during their incarceration, as many of the inmates involved in the *Bad Boys Bakery* went on to secure employment in the baking industry after the show aired.

Regrettably, in the late 2010s, the bakery ceased operating as the company that ran the operations stopped attempting to finance it. But the Bad Boys Bakery reopened its doors (not literally, it's in a prison) in November 2022 and began trading under the sponsorship of the Clink Charity. The charity works to provide prisoners with meaningful tasks during their time in prison and runs several restaurants alongside 30 prison kitchens where prisoners prepare meals for the public to enjoy.

SHARING A POOL
TO FIGHT RACISM

Fred Rogers, AKA Mr. Rogers, was an iconic and beloved children's TV host whose career on the small screen ran from 1968 to 2001 on the show *Mister Rogers' Neighborhood*. If you know anything about this show, then you'd be right in thinking that the whole thing would serve nicely as an uplifting story.

Mister Rogers had a tough childhood, affected by bullying and his introverted nature. He would indulge himself in make-believe, speaking with his ventriloquist puppet and stuffed toys as much as he could. In his early years, he created his own world where there wasn't the cruelty that he was experiencing in his normal life. He went on to work as a Presbyterian minister and became an accomplished musician, excelling at the piano. It was after his ordainment that he pursued a career educating children through TV.

Mister Rogers' Neighborhood was a show aimed at teaching kids about subjects they may find confusing or upsetting. The show achieved such longevity due to Rogers' ability to take something complicated and present it in an easy-to-digest form for his young audience. The show ran at a slow pace, with some light whimsy and a few jokes, but it was mainly about providing a space to model kindness.

In 1969, a now-famous episode aired on PBS that many critics have hailed as an important moment in negotiating race relations in the US. Officer Clemmons was a recurring character on the show, an actor portraying a Black police officer who kept order within the eponymous neighborhood. In itself, this was important. By demonstrating that anyone of any background can be an important figure in their community, societal barriers were dismantled for children who watched the show. During the episode, Rogers invites Clemmons to cool off by putting his feet in a small pool alongside Rogers.

The moment may seem small, almost unworthy of note. But in 1969, swimming pools were still segregated in many parts of America, and Black people were not allowed to swim alongside their White peers. By sharing the small pool with Clemmons, Rogers demonstrated to children (as well as adults) that love and friendship don't know any color boundaries.

The legacy of this single episode cannot be understated. The show was immensely popular, and children from varied socio-economic backgrounds watched it. Witnessing such kindness on the show sowed the seeds for empathy in the next generations and has helped America move away from the problematic attitudes of the 1960s.

CHANGING LIFE FOR BLIND PEOPLE FOREVER

There are many difficulties in life for blind people. The world is built for people who can see, and blind people can have a tough time navigating the complexities that come with not having functioning vision. Reading, however, is made accessible through the use of braille. If you're not sure what braille is, it's a series of raised dots that allow blind people to read through using their fingertips.

(Braille looks a bit like this)

Braille's invention, which allowed blind people to read and take in information without listening to it, was a huge moment for people with serious visual impairments. Its invention is a remarkable story that begins with one young boy born in 1809.

The boy's name was Louis Braille, and he was born in a small village near Paris, France. Louis injured himself at the age of three when playing with his father's tools, and gradually lost his sight due to the ensuing infection. Louis was a bright child and attended the National Institute for Blind Youth in Paris but found the schooling to be difficult to access. It relied on large books with raised lettering, which proved difficult to read. When he was just 12 years old, Louis learned of a communication system used by the French Army in the dark called "night writing." The system used raised dots that could be understood without sight. However, it was exceptionally complex and too difficult for the layperson to use reliably.

So, Louis got to work. He wanted a system that worked in the same way as the night writing but was simpler to grasp. He developed his own tools as he punched dots into thick paper, experimenting with different groupings of dots to form different letters and words. He tirelessly worked on his new invention for three years until he presented braille to the National Institute for Blind Youth in 1824, aged 15.

The invention was very quickly a success and was adopted across the world as the preferred reading and writing method for blind people. Braille was so successful precisely because it took up less room than previous forms of writing. The days of requiring huge books with oversized, raised letters were gone; instead, a book made from braille was not much larger than a typed book. It was now more portable and practical, and as such became a vital tool for education and communication all over the world.

THE MAN WITH
THE GOLDEN ARM

Millions of us will need blood at some stage of our lives. Whether it's due to an unlucky injury or an illness that requires a transfusion, having a decent supply of blood saves lives. The number of blood donors is rising worldwide, as more and more people recognize the necessity to donate blood when healthy. Yet the overall figures are still way behind what is needed. Somewhere around 7% of Americans are actively donating blood and one in 30 Australians donate blood. In Europe, the figures are better, with 37% of Europeans having donated or actively donating (in Austria, two-thirds of the population are proudly part of that number). Ultimately, we do need more.

In particular, the world needs more people with rare blood types or with specific antibodies that help fight illnesses to donate. For instance, someone like James Harrison, who born in Australia in 1951. Harrison underwent serious surgery in his youth and only survived due to the large amount of blood that was available for him during the procedure. When he learned what saved his life, he vowed to donate after he turned 18.

After his first few donations, his blood was analyzed and it was found, remarkably, that his blood contained antibodies that can be used to prevent blood conditions in newborn infants. This was fantastic news on two levels because 1) young children's lives would be saved by his donations and 2) the antibodies could be harvested through his plasma, which can be safely donated every two weeks.

Harrison went on to donate 1,173 times, the last being in 2018, when he was forced to retire, as 81 years old remains the cut-off for blood or plasma donation. Over the years of donating, it's estimated that Harrison managed to save more than two million babies' lives through his generosity. He received the Medal of The Order of Australia in 1999 as well as being nominated for the New South Wales Local Hero division of the Australian of the Year awards in 2011. He has since been dubbed "The Man with the Golden Arm" but remains humble about his accomplishment:

"I could say it's the only record that I hope is broken, because if they do, they have donated a thousand donations."

THE MIRACLE
ON THE HUDSON

It's amazing how much of a hazard birds can be to our holiday plans. One single bird has the potential to force a plane to land, or take out an engine, thus both ruining your trip to Mexico and ending the bird's life, a double whammy. In 2009, the world watched on in amazement as pilot Chesley "Sully" Sullenberger managed to circumnavigate this very issue and saved the lives of 155 people.

The date was January 15, 2009, and Sully was piloting a US Airways flight from New York City to Charlotte and Seattle alongside his co-pilot, Jeffrey Skiles. The flight would normally be unremarkable, a routinely performed operation. However, within a few minutes of take-off, the pilot and co-pilot both heard a loud thud. They had collided with a flock of birds, disabling both engines!

Pilots are trained to deal with emergency situations, as rare as they are, and both Sully and Jeffrey quickly came to the decision that they had no way of reaching an airport with no engines. Sully decided that the only plausible place in New York City that could accommodate a large jet was the Hudson River. Sully calmly told the passengers to *"brace for impact"*, and the passengers prepared for the worst; within seconds, the plane crash-landed into the Hudson River.

After the impact, the crew and passengers exhaled, taking a moment to look around at what they assumed would be wreckage. Bizarrely, all seemed relatively okay. The plane had landed without any major complications; the impact did cause injuries to a handful of passengers, but the majority were completely fine. Boats were quickly sent to the floating plane, and they removed the people from the floating vessel. News stations rushed to cover the story, the tone shifting from despair to amazement as the remarkable tale unraveled.

Sully became an overnight hero, with the story becoming known as "The Miracle on the Hudson." In 2016, a film was made based on the story, called *Sully* and starring Tom Hanks. Sully remained humble throughout, refusing to let the sudden fame go to his head. He even found time to give people some helpful tips for dealing with a crisis:

> *"Having a plan enabled us to keep our hope alive. Perhaps similarly, people who are in their personal crises can be reminded that no matter how dire the circumstance, or how little time you have to deal with it, further action is always possible. There's always a way out of even the tightest spot."*

IT'S BETTER THAN
A BIRTHDAY CARD!

The Apollo space missions, launched by NASA between 1968 and 1972, remain the vision of optimistic space exploration even five decades after they ended. The Apollo missions brought humans to the moon for the first time, producing the infinitely famous Neil Armstrong line, *"That's one small step for man, one giant leap for mankind."* The missions were inspiring on their own; they marked the start of humanity's obsession with exploring and investigating. When Armstrong made it to the moon, the possibilities seemed infinite. Where would humans go next?

Upsettingly, since the end of the program, people haven't returned to the moon. The last man to have visited the moon spent 75 hours there, the longest of any astronaut. His name was Eugene Cernan, and he's left a legacy on the surface that remains some 50 years later.

Cernan departed Earth with the Apollo 17 crew in December 1972, aware that this would be the last visit to the moon for some time. Cernan journeyed to the moon alongside Harrison Schmitt and Ronald Evans. He spent three days on the lunar surface with Schmitt, while Evans orbited above in the command module.

Cernan spent his time on the moon conducting some very serious experiments, as you might expect a NASA astronaut to do. He conducted geological surveys that helped bring a greater understanding of the moon's history - and he also completed a few tasks that NASA hadn't asked him to do. Cernan wanted to mark the occasion as well as the end of the Apollo missions, so he first ensured that he'd left a footprint on the moon's surface. Once this was done, he then carved his daughter's initials into the lunar dust, alongside "TDC." The latter stands for the Texas Dental Center, the institute where his wife was training back on Earth.

Cernan left the moon on 14 December 1972 with a poignant message about humankind's future space exploration and the everlasting quest for knowledge. He lived until he was 82, dying in 2017. He wouldn't have expected that he'd remain the last person on the moon at the time of his death, but he would have been encouraged by the work being done elsewhere in our Solar System. In Cernan's words:

> "America's challenge of today has forged man's destiny of tomorrow. And, as we leave the Moon at Taurus-Littrow, we leave as we came and, God willing, as we shall return, with peace and hope for all mankind. Godspeed the crew of Apollo 17."

THE LORD OF FISH
AND ALL THINGS WATERY

Is it possible to be a valuable member of the military if you are unable to hold a gun? How about if you're unable to discern who is a friend or foe? What if you have an almost insatiable addiction to fish?

All of these things are true of Nils Olav III, who currently holds the rank of Colonel-in-Chief of the Norwegian King's Guard. Nils Olav III, of course, inherited the role from Nils Olav II; who in turn took on the job from Nils Olav I. The role of Colonel-in-Chief was first awarded to Nils Olav in 1972, and he remains the first King Penguin to hold the rank. That's right, he's a penguin!

The truth is that the Scottish Penguin Nils Olavs will have held this role ever since 1972, and their shared accolades have only grown as the years pass by. Nils Olav was a beloved penguin in the 20th century, seen as a hilarious and cute mascot of the King's Guard. In 2008, as Nils Olav II had taken over, the King of Norway knighted him. A specially made tuxedo was crafted for Nils Olav II, and he received the medal and sword of the Royal Norwegian Guard, making him the first penguin to do so. Hundreds of guests attended the ceremony, watching on as Nils

Olav II inspected the guard and listened to a speech from the King:

"[Nils is] in every way qualified to receive the honor and dignity of knighthood."

The accolades don't stop coming for Sir Nils Olav as in 2016, the knight of the realm was promoted to the role of brigadier, in a ceremony attended by members of the King's Guard. At this current stage, Sir Nils Olav III outranks Nils Egelien, who started the whole practice of honoring the penguin in the first place!

Nils Egelien suggested that the regiment of the Norwegian King's Guard adopt a penguin from Edinburgh Zoo in 1972. He named the penguin after himself (Nils) and King Olav V (Olav).

The story is quite laughable. The Nils Olavs will continue to receive higher and higher honors as time goes by. New Nils Olavs will be chosen, inheriting the roles and successes of those who waddled before them. But the story highlights the importance of tradition, as well as the power of a good mascot. People enjoy visiting Nils Olav, who resides in Edinburgh Zoo and find his story very amusing. What more can we ask for than a penguin who holds higher office than 99% of the people in his country?

PERHAPS IT'S JUST
A REALLY HAIRY MAN?

Throughout the 20th century there's been a preoccupation among some people around two types of creatures, the Yeti and Bigfoot. The theory is that both creatures are rare, large, bipedal, hairy, man-like animals that roam two distinct areas of the Earth.

Legend has it that the Yeti inhabits the snowy peaks of the Himalayas, a mountain range that remains difficult to access for humans. The Yeti is said to be covered from head-to-toe in thick fur that provides camouflage in its almost permanently snowy environment. Meanwhile, Bigfoot is rumored to live in the forests and mountains of North America, its appearance is said to be similar but darker in color to blend into Canada's deep forests better.

The Yeti is supposedly apelike, hunched, and smaller. Bigfoot reportedly stands somewhere between seven to nine feet tall and is broad across the shoulders. Bigfoot is supposedly shy by nature, hence it being borderline impossible to spot; while the Yeti routinely wanders into Sherpa villages around the Himalayas, searching for food.

"Why is this book telling me about two creatures that almost definitely don't exist?"

Good question! The reason is that the ongoing amateur investigations into the existence of these undiscovered creatures speak to many joyous aspects of the human psyche. An entire field of research has developed to study creatures that are believed to exist but without proof, called "cryptozoology." Groups such as the Bigfoot Field Researchers Organization and The International Cryptozoology Museum have emerged to legitimize the studying of our long-lost cousins. They work with eyewitnesses, researchers, and other interested parties to gather information.

In response, some scientists and skeptics also hold an interest in the study of animals that may not exist. These cryptozoologist-skeptics conduct their own investigations and experiments to debunk the "findings" of the groups mentioned above.

The stories that emerge around Bigfoot and the Yeti are fun to investigate; whether it be a single hunter who saw a paw print that didn't look quite right, or an amateur explorer who claims to have taken a picture of a Yeti while scaling a mountain. These stories tell the tale of humans looking to solve one of the last mysteries in our meticulously-explored planet.

You'll have your own opinion as to whether creatures such as the Yeti or Bigfoot exist. Regardless, it's fun to acknowledge the hard work going into something that may all be a complete waste of time.

NETHERLANDS' VILLAGE
FOR THOSE LOST IN TIME

Unfortunately, many of us will know someone who goes on to have dementia in their lifetime. Currently, ten million people are diagnosed every year, and though there are encouraging developments in the pharmaceutical field, there's no cure yet. Dementia is a condition that involves a progressive loss of brain function, usually related to memory. In most countries, being diagnosed with dementia is essentially a diagnosis of being placed in a "care home" somewhere down the line.

The Netherlands, however, has undertaken a different strategy to help patients with dementia by creating a "village" for sufferers. The village, called De Hogeweyk, was created by Dr Hogeweyk and opened in 2009, spawning copycat projects around the world.

The facility is designed to look and function like a regular village; there are streets, restaurants, shops, and houses. The idea of the village, which sits in Weesp near Amsterdam, is to create an environment that Dutch people living with dementia will find familiar. The village is easily navigable with a manufactured calm environment, which helps reduce stress for the patients who struggle in busier population centers.

The houses accommodate somewhere between six to eight patients, with full-time staff provided to help with maintaining the household. The residents are permitted to provide some decoration to their house, increasing buy-in. The houses are located near amenities such as a hair salon, a supermarket, restaurants, and even a theater; interconnected paths keep residents active, especially important for dementia sufferers.

There are myriad reasons for De Hogeweyk's success. The excellent care from well-paid nurses certainly helps, but the sense of community that's developed in the village is also pivotal. Socialization is encouraged, group activities are organized, and everyday tasks are carried out by the citizens. The sense of "normal" independence continues for many of the patients, which can be really important for their state of mid as they fight the illness.

Dementia is a horrific illness, and those burdened with it suffer greatly, but De Hogeweyk has received international commendations for its respectful care. Many governments across the world are looking into creating similar programs in their country, or have already agreed to them.

THERE'S OVERACHIEVING, THEN THERE'S THAT!

Emma Yang was just 12 years old when her grandmother received a diagnosis of Alzheimer's, a form of dementia that particularly targets memory. Emma watched as the illness slowly affected her grandmother in a variety of ways, as well as the greater impact on her family who supported her.

Emma was an academically impressive student. She'd been coding since she was six years old, and her teachers were well aware of her potential. She decided that she wanted to use her knowledge of coding and app development to create an app that helped Alzheimer's sufferers live with their condition. By the age of 14, she was well underway to launching 'Timeless'.

Timeless hasn't just had input from Emma and the experience with her grandmother. The app has also received input from a litany of experts on Alzheimer's. It is designed to be a simple way for Alzheimer's patients to track events, stay connected to family members, and help recognize people through facial recognition technology. The app is accessible to caregivers, patients, and friends/family members, providing a digital social space for all involved.

Emma has received international recognition for her work on the app and is the recipient of an inordinate amount of grants and awards for her innovative work. She has given a TEDx talk, has performed at Carnegie Hall three times, and is seen as one of the world's defining young entrepreneurs.

Physicians around the world recommend Timeless to their patients and their families. It's inspiring enough to know that consistent work is being carried out to make the lives of Alzheimer's sufferers easier. It's even more inspiring to see teenagers making the biggest strides of all. It speaks to the generosity and humility of some of our younger generations, who want to see a greater future for their world.

FRAUD? OR JUST
BEING SMART?

This is a story that emphasizes humankind's bare-faced cheek and about how, given the chance, most of us would take the opportunity to make a lot of money.

In 1984, the game-show *Press Your Luck* was host to a remarkable televisual event when one contestant, Michael Larson, won the most money anyone had ever won on the show before. *Press Your Luck* features a board and "randomizer" that provides the contestant with a random amount of money to win. The key, however, is that this isn't random. The randomizer consisted of five patterns that it repeated, but most people wouldn't have noticed that.

However, Michael Larson isn't "most people." He used his VCR to record episodes of *Press Your Luck* after its premiere in 1983 and observed the distinct patterns from the randomizer. He became increasingly confident that he could predict exactly where the randomizer would land. Some rigorous testing on his own homemade board confirmed that he could keep control of the board indefinitely if he simply followed the patterns.

Larson saved up his money and flew to Los Angeles, where he auditioned for the show. The studio accepted him for recording, despite the customer supervisor being suspicious of Larson, and he prepared for the filming.

He employed his strategy perfectly, expertly retaining control of the show and racking up a small fortune. Larson's success lengthened the show so much that, for the first time, it had to be shown over two episodes. Eventually, he walked away from the studio having won the modern-day equivalent of $290,000!

Of course, the studio was furious. They were convinced that Larson was cheating and refused to hand the fortune to him; however, the lawyers could find no legitimate reason to deny him the money. Larson hadn't altered the game at all; he'd just been intelligent enough to figure out how to work it. The studio forked over the cash and told Larson to never come back.

In the end, Larson squandered most of the money, but there's something pleasingly amusing about a normal man winning big at the expense of a wealthy TV studio. It's worth pointing out that it's cases like this that make game-shows think more carefully about how they operate, so you're unlikely to find a similar exploit. But if you do, then good luck to you. Just remember to *pretend* that you didn't know what you were doing.

THE GREAT GULABI GANG

In 2006, a superhero group emerged from the dust of violence and abuse. The group continues to stand up for what is correct, fighting against corruption and misdeeds where they see it. We're not talking about the release of *X-Men: The Last Stand*. We're instead talking about the Gulabi Gang, who operate in the Banda District, Uttar Pradesh, India.

The Gulabi Gang are so called because their name literally means Pink Gang, a reference to the pink saris that the members wear. The group is entirely made up of women activists, and they fight for the rights of women across India. They currently have approximately 300,000 members. Sampat Pal Devi founded the Gulabi Gang. The former child bride and mother to five had witnessed the mistreatment of women in her community all her life. She'd suffered abuse as a child and felt that standards imposed on women were not necessarily the same for men.

The Banda District has a high rate of violence toward women, a low female literacy rate, and high reports of forced child marriage. As well as this, the region is dictated greatly by the caste system, a class system within India that subjugates certain people based on their race. The Gulabi Gang took to the district, adorned in pink saris and wielding bamboo sticks as a weapon.

The Gang knew full well that they would face opposition, which they had happen. Many politicians have spoken out against the threat of the Gulabi Gang, fearing it may compromise traditional gender roles. Their violent acts have also been condemned, though the Gang employs these only as a last resort. The Gang uses their sticks to thrash men who are enacting domestic or sexual violence; they first ask the offender to stop and, if that fails, beat him into stopping. The group maintains that this is uncommon, and they're only punishing the men as the police fail to.

"If a woman seeks the membership of Gulabi Gang, it is because she has suffered injustice, has been oppressed and does not see any other recourse. All our women can stand up to the men and if need be, seek retribution through lathis [bamboo sticks]."

The group has advocated for women in the region since 2006. They have sought financial independence for women, as well as to improve the education provided for women. The group set up a school in 2008, which 800 girls attend. The gang visits families to encourage them to send their female children to schooling and onto further education such as university or college.

It's emboldening to hear of people standing up for what is correct, or righteous, in the face of inequality. Perhaps more than this, picturing women smacking an abuser with a large stick while all dressed in pink, brings a smile to the face.

THIS IS HARLEY
A LAUGHING MATTER

Have you ever seen the *Sons of Anarchy*? It's a show about a violent biker gang that gained enormous popularity at the start of the 2010s. It helped solidify the image of bikers as uber-masculine, bearded outlaws who care for brotherhood and are scary. The image holds true with many bikers, and their presence can be intimidating for some. The long beards, leather, and tattoos aren't symbols that traditionally come to mind when we hear the phrase "care in the community."

Bikers know that they have a slightly fearsome reputation, but many recognize that they can use this for good. This is why the organization Bikers Against Child Abuse (BACA) was founded in Utah, in 1995. The group's primary mission is to create a safe environment for children who may have been abused by providing them with security, safety, and support. BACA does this by being a visible presence in the child's life while acting as a role model for all involved.

BACA doesn't work alone, of course. They work closely with local authorities and law enforcement agencies to assist the children, especially as the children are vulnerable and need considered care. Once a child is referred to BACA, the group assigns a group of bikers (usually ensuring male and female are present) who become the child's "guardians of the night." The group promises the child that if they feel afraid or threatened, they can call on their "guardians" for support.

The members must go through a screening process before being accepted as members, including criminal background checks and extensive training. The members commit themselves to be available to the child that they're assigned to, knowing that they may need to step in to provide security in potentially dangerous situations.

The group participates in community events, wanting to be seen as a positive presence wherever their chapter is situated. They have been known to fundraise through charity rides, help prevent bullying in schools, and accompany children to school or anywhere they may feel vulnerable. Ultimately, the group may look scary, but inside they are big softies who want to make the world better for all children.

The group receives a lot of praise in the media for their hard work, and the organization has grown over the years, now active in 18 different countries globally. The group aims to help victimized children regain their sense of self-worth and feel safe again. Their dedication to valuable charity work has helped many children move on with their lives through love, care, and managing fear.

If you want to learn more about BACA, then visit www.bacaworld.org to learn more.

THE EVERLASTING LEGACY OF HARRIET TUBMAN

If you're an American reading this book, you very likely have a good idea of who Harriet Tubman is. Tubman is a celebrated figure in American history, dramatically influencing the abolition of slavery in the country and being present in the early movements for civil rights. Her life is dramatic, interesting, and inspiring.

Tubman was born into slavery in Maryland in the 1820s. She spent her childhood working as a slave in the household before being transferred to fieldwork. Even in her early teens, Tubman possessed a fire within her. The fire yearned for the correct treatment of her peers and for the barbarity of slavery to end. Tubman herself suffered a great injury when her head was struck by an angry overseer wielding a two-pound weight.

Tubman escaped her bondage in 1849, fleeing to the Northern states of America where slavery had been abolished and joining the Underground Railroad. The railroad wasn't a real railroad but a network of abolitionists who worked effortlessly to transport enslaved people from the South to the North to be free. Being part of the network was dangerous. Members of the Underground Railroad had been shot for their participation and there was never any guarantee that you'd be successful in your endeavors.

Tubman was instrumental to the railroad's success. She visited the South in 1850, helping her family escape their imprisonment. This first trip was crucial, proving to Tubman that if she could rescue her family, then she could rescue others. She continued to journey South, risking her life each time to help guide other enslaved people toward freedom; Tubman earned the nickname 'Moses' for her leadership and ability to lead others. Her experiences as an enslaved person, as well as her work for the railroad, made her a figurehead of the abolitionist movement. Tubman claimed to have rescued more than 300 people from slavery and never lost a single one on her journey.

Tubman continued to fight for equality after the Underground Railroad, leading expeditions to free more people during the Civil War during the 1860s. She worked as a nurse, as well as a spy, helping gather intelligence for the Union Army.

Tubman went on to fight for women's suffrage, leading campaigns for women's right to vote. Her already strong reputation as an abolitionist helped the movement gain further legitimacy. She went on to operate a home for elderly African Americans later in her life, providing care for those in need.

Tubman's legacy has been retold in hundreds of books, movies, and TV shows. She's an important part of American history, providing a great insight into how someone who was born into an impossible situation fought to change the world.

WHEN IT RAINS IT POURS, AND WHEN IT'S SUNNY IT'S A HEATWAVE

They say that bad things come in threes. The idea is that if your car has broken down and now, you're late for work, then you'll be lumbered with unpaid overtime on the weekend when you get there. It's not the most positive way of thinking about things, sure, but we can all relate to occasions where it's felt like the whole world is against us. For Geraldine Gimblet, 74, this was the case when her daughter was diagnosed with cancer.

Geraldine's daughter, Lawrencina, was a middle-aged woman with some funds to contribute toward her care, but the funds required far outstripped her means. Geraldine didn't waste a minute and donated her entire life savings to help Lawrencina fight the disease. Geraldine's generosity came without even a moment's hesitation. She had no concern for her years of retirement left: the most important thing was to ensure that her daughter lived to see the other side of being sick. If bad things do come in threes, then Geraldine had one more coming her way. (1) her daughter was incredibly sick and (2) she now had little to no money beyond her pension.

"I really didn't think about it. I just did what I had to do."

In April 2023, Lawrencina completed her last treatment for breast cancer, winning the battle with the support of her mother. Geraldine was naturally ecstatic for her daughter and on her way home, decided to buy herself a lottery ticket, especially as luck seemed to be on her side.

The $10 ticket was worth $2m. Initially, she had to get Lawrencina to check on her phone, to make sure that Geraldine wasn't imagining things; but after a brief check and a phone call, it was confirmed. Geraldine chose to receive the prize in one lump sum, leaving her with $1.6m after tax.

Perhaps if bad things do come in threes, good things do as well. (1) Geraldine's daughter rings the bell at the hospital, signifying the end of treatment and (2) Geraldine wins $1.6m in the lottery. One wonders if there's a (3) on the way, and if there is, just how much a loving, hard-working mother deserves it.

ATTEMPTED ASSASSINATION AT 15, NOBEL PRIZE AT 17

Some people need very little introduction, and Malala Yousafzai is one of them. If you've been aware of even half of her story, you'd be aware of her remarkable perseverance and bravery in the face of evil depravity. If you aren't aware of Malala's incredible story, then the following account will briefly introduce you to the work she has done *so far* in her young life.

Malala was born in 1997 in Mingora, a small town in Pakistan. Malala's father encouraged her to pursue education and self-improvement, being a schoolmaster himself. She was a bright student and excelled in her schooling. She adored reading and loved her time at school. This was cut short when, in 2007, the Taliban took control of the Swat Valley, where Malala lived.

The Taliban is an extremist Islamic group that fundamentally disagrees with many beliefs and rights that people all over the world take for granted. When the Taliban took control of Malala's home, they banned girls' education, ripping apart Malala's world and taking from her what she enjoyed the most. Malala and her father were furious and spoke out against the unjust laws that had been foisted upon them.

Malala blogged anonymously for the BBC in 2008 at just 11 years old. She wrote about the difficulties of being a schoolgirl under Taliban rule and of the day-to-day atrocities in the region. She even appeared, anonymously, on TV, discussing the separation of her family and how much she missed the life that had ceased to exist. Eventually, the Taliban figured out who was contributing to the blog and, in 2012, an assassination attempt was organized.

Malala, seen as a threat to the Taliban's control, was shot at the age of 15, while on the bus to take her exams. Her injuries were serious, and she needed immediate brain surgery to keep her alive. Offers of medical treatment came from around the world, but she was ultimately sent to England for the bulk of her care. Malala woke from her coma almost three months after the shooting and began writing her book *I Am Malala: The Girl Who Stood Up for Education and was Shot by the Taliban,* which was published in 2013.

The book was an international phenomenon and the shooting of an already popular figure caused widespread protests in Pakistan, as well as drawing the global eye to the ongoing conflict in the country. Pakistan faced calls from the UN to ensure education was being delivered appropriately for all children, and money was donated by governments and common folk alike to help. Meanwhile, Malala finished her education in England, graduating with a stellar set of results in 2017 before furthering her studies at Oxford University.

Malala has been a continued advocate for universal education and has spoken with several politicians around the world about what work still needs to be done. Her activism continues to bring attention to an issue that, for some, is barely a consideration. Malala has shown that in the face of adversity, one has no option but to keep on fighting. Her legacy will continue to inspire the next generation of politically active young people, who inherit a better, safer Pakistan than Malala did.

THE SOLAR MAMAS

On Earth, 1.1 billion people live without access to power. As a result, when the sun sets in the evening, they are in the dark. All work and learning must cease and the main option in most places is to sleep. In most communities where there is no available power, the only alternative is to use lamps that burn fuel such as kerosene. These lamps emit harmful levels of air pollution that negatively affect the fight against climate change as well as the users' health. A lot of work needs to be done to bring these communities power, and ideally, it would be done without causing greater damage to our planet.

Luckily, there are some solutions. Solar power has become one of the world's dominant power sources after fossil fuels. Solar power is nothing new; its history traces back almost 70 years, and solar panels have been in use for much of the 21st century. But it seems both sensible and useful to provide solar power where possible, especially if starting from scratch.

This is the logic that Barefoot College employs. The college is an international, woman-centered, global network that works to develop rural communities. They currently operate in over 90 countries and their work is bringing great success to areas that would have little to no chance without them.

The college runs a six-month training program where women are trained in how to install and maintain solar panels and lamps, which bring electricity and light to the community. The course also educates women in other areas such as financial management, health education, reproductive health, and the use of technology in their day-to-day lives. The work helps empower women in rural, poor communities, who are often coming from a position where their opportunities to work outside the home are limited.

The college has received funding from a variety of donors, such as UN Women, Coca-Cola, and Hogan Lovells, to keep the programs running and to hopefully work on the expansion. The empowerment being gifted to women by the college through education is helping power their world for the future.

Florentina Choc, from Belize, had this to say about the program:

> "In my village, there are 68 households. All the panels and lights for these homes, I installed... Once I brought light to my community, I could see it. Something changed in the village, not like before when we stayed in the dark. Now my village has light."

THE BOY WHO
HARNESSED THE WIND

For many people on our planet, it doesn't take much to bring tough times to their community. In Malawi, many families live harvest-to-harvest. This means they rely on the food and money that arrive from their crop harvest each year. If there's a problem with that harvest, then there's a problem with their stream of income.

For 14-year-old William Kamkwamba's family in Malawi, this was the case in 2001 when a failing crop and famine threatened to devastate his entire community. William was an inspired pupil at school and had promise, but his family had to pull him out of education as they didn't have the funds to spare given the emergency situation with their crop yield. He spent his spare time reading at the school's library and scavenging for scraps of metal, wire, or anything else of use.

William had become infatuated with electronics while reading at the library, and he was especially interested in wind turbines. He was sure that if his family had one, their lives would drastically change for the better. Unfortunately, turbines are both difficult to get hold of in rural Malawi and expensive. He decided that he'd build his own.

Months went by as William worked by lamp-light into the early hours of the morning, desperately trying to make a working prototype for his turbine. His neighbors discredited the effort, thinking that it was misplaced given they were suffering a famine, but William was undeterred. When he was ready, he hooked up the turbine to a small car battery and, to his amazement, it worked! He had used the wind to generate power for his home.

Local farmers were amazed that the turbine worked. William's family were now able to read books after dark and had more hours of light for their education. The news spread further, to the *Daily Times* in Malawi at first, then to the director at TED, who asked William to talk at one of their conferences. The fame spiraled, with offers from venture capitalists flooding in to fund his further education, and money being donated for further work to be done in Malawi to bring power to numerous poorer communities.

William went on to write a book called *The Boy Who Harnessed The Wind* in 2013, as well as being part of a documentary called *William and the Windmill* that same year. The international recognition received by William has brought him renown and money, which he pumps back into Malawi, funding schools and helping young people access education. He continues to inspire the Malawian youth and holds talks around the world on the importance of innovating in the face of climate change, trying to inspire others to do the same:

"I would tell most young people that in life you can go through many difficulties, but if you know what you want to do, if you can focus, and work, then in the end, you will end up doing it."

THE HIGHEST COURT
IN ALL THE LAND

The US Supreme Court is the most important (highest) court in the USA. Once a decision has been made within the Supreme Court, it's generally final. There's no one else to complain to after that; it's the end of the line. As such, the Court is a very serious building where decisions are made by very serious people. In its history, the US Supreme Court has heard cases about the civil rights of Black Americans, the right for a woman to access abortion, and serious corruption charges against politicians.

As you can imagine, working in the institution is difficult, stressful, and requires acting with the utmost propriety. For this exact reason, another court was made that sits above the Supreme Court. Literally. There's a basketball court in the room above the courtroom!

The reason for the "Highest Court in all the Land" was to give the clerks and justices a way to unwind when on their breaks. The court is a full-size regulation court, with incredible views of the Capitol building. The center spot has the Supreme Court's seal in it and the backboards are made of clear plexiglass. Needless to say, it's a nice place to shoot some hoops, and many have done.

Supreme Court Justices have played there, with some judges in the court today going on record to say they enjoy a trip to the fifth-floor exercise center as often as possible. Many unverifiable and legendary stories accompany the space. Supposedly, a group of visiting dignitaries were brought up to the court to sink some hoops, and a junior clerk was playing with them. The clerk was exceptionally impressive in the game and the dignitaries asked for his name, and he coolly responded "Just another lawyer."

Charity games have been held on the court, but these are rare. Generally speaking, unless you work there, or are *very* important, you won't get a chance to visit the court. But who knows, perhaps if you work really hard and become a lawyer within the most important court in all of America, you'll get a chance to visit the Highest Court in all of America.

CHILEAN MINERS RESCUE

If you're of an age that means 2010 isn't a time of vague, misremembered history, then it's likely you'll remember the Copiapó mining accident, or "the Chilean mining accident." The story was international news and was later even made into a movie called *33*. The basic story is that 33 miners from Chile became trapped in a mine and after first being presumed dead, survived for 69 days under the surface before they were rescued.

Chile has a history of mining, being the world's major producer of copper, which is commonly used in many electronics and gadgets across the planet. Mining is a dangerous profession, and the industry in Chile is no exception. Approximately 34 people die every year mining in Chile. The job can only be made as safe as they can; accidents do happen. Accidents also seemed to happen an inordinate amount at San Esteban Mining Company, which had received dozens of fines for breaching safety regulations in the years before the famed incident.

The mine collapsed on August 5, 2010. A driver was able to escape the mine quickly as it caved in, but 33 other men were stuck inside. They attempted to escape through ventilation shafts, but the ladders required (by law) to be present were not there. Drills were used to access the area thought to contain the miners' bodies. On August 22, the drill emerged after successfully reaching the area...with a note attached to it!

"Estamos bien en el refugio los 33"
(All 33 of us are fine in the shelter)

The news of the miners' survival was met with international celebration and the rescue operation began.

The miners had a very small amount of canned food and bottled water. They were only able to survive the first 17 days through careful rationing and keeping a cool head despite the gravity of the situation. By the time they'd been found, the men had lost approximately 17 pounds in weight.

Once they'd been found, further rations were delivered to the men, and they were told that rescue was likely. So, the men entertained themselves however they could. They could take walks along the 1.2-mile-long tunnel they had access to, play games, cook dinner, or mock each other about the gifts they received from family members above ground.

As the rescue neared its end, the miners' families gathered at the surface. Reporters from all over the globe had their cameras trained on the exit from which the miners would emerge. The miners surfaced wearing sunglasses and "Gracias Senor" t-shirts to an incredible reception. Well, apart from Florencio Avalos, who was told off by his wife for failing to shave!

The miners were treated as minor celebrities. They were interviewed countless times, received a paid-for trip to

Disneyland, and one of the miners wrote a book about their experiences. The company was sued for their negligence and the families of the miners received a sum of money for the ordeal. The most incredible aspect of the entire story is the miners' ability to keep their spirits high even in the face of a potentially terrifying demise. It speaks volumes about our capacity to keep on keeping on.

THE RISE OF MEDELLIN

Many people are aware of Pablo Escobar and his drug empire that ran throughout the 20th century. Escobar was a drug lord from Colombia; he illegally exported cocaine across the world while making a colossal amount of money in the process. Some people have fond memories of Escobar because of the money he helped bring into Colombia, but Escobar's business also brought death wherever it reached. This was no truer than in Medellin.

Medellin is the second-largest city in Colombia and had a reputation for decades as one of the world's most dangerous cities. The drug cartels were in control for a long time, with drug-related violence ever-present and law enforcement ill-equipped to deal with the situation. During the 21st century, however, Medellin has undergone a dramatic transformation.

Since the toppling of Escobar's drug empire, Medellin has invested a lot of money into its public infrastructure. New public transportation, parks, and cultural centers have been developed to make the city more interconnected and pleasurable to be in. The residents have had a voice in the re-development of the city, offering their opinions on what needs improving, which has only improved community engagement in the once-troubled city.

The poverty-stricken neighborhoods of Medellin have had a particular focus. Even after the departure of Escobar, these communities have dealt with serious drug-related violence and health problems. The greater focus on art projects and infrastructure has helped build a sense of pride in the community and has driven violence away. The poorer districts have received a tremendous investment in education at all levels as well, with new research centers and universities providing options beyond poverty.

In 2013, the *Wall Street Journal* voted Medellin as the "Most Innovative City of the Year," in recognition of the hard work by the residents that's improved life for millions. There's some way to go yet, but the city is a testament to not giving in or merely accepting a lost cause. Very few people would visit Medellin in the 1990s, but today it thrives and will continue to do so as long as it's supported.

PRESIDENTIAL SWEET

Politicians frequently find themselves under the microscope; it's the nature of their job. Politicians' sole job is to improve the country in which they've been elected, be that on a smaller or grander scale. Their effectiveness can be judged in terms of economic recovery, approval ratings, or by an innumerable number of other metrics. But how about generosity?

Jose Mujica was the president of Uruguay from 2010 to 2015 and has garnered a reputation as a kind-hearted, progressive leader that many Uruguayans miss. The BBC described Mujica as humble in an article titled, "The World's Poorest President," and the *Guardian UK* praised his "no frills" approach.

The reason for the plaudits from media outlets is predominantly due to Mujica's decision at the start of his Presidency to donate 90% of his salary to charity. He refused the luxury of the Presidential palace and the staff that comes with that, instead opting for a modest property that he and his wife have shared since 2005. Mujica felt that given that he and his wife didn't have children, they have no need for a vast income, but live happily on what they need. Mujica drives a 1987 Volkswagen Beetle that is valued at $1,800. In 2014, he was informed by the press that an offer of $1m had been proposed to purchase it from him. Mujica declared that if the sale were to happen, the money would have to go to a homeless charity that he patronized.

Mujica has been a proponent of left-wing politics for the 21st century, and his presidency saw the legalization of same-sex marriage in 2013, bringing international support for the politician. He felt that South America's problem with illegal drugs should be funded by the legalization of marijuana, adopting a similar program to Canada and some states in the USA. The money through the sale of marijuana goes to rehabilitation clinics and helps people fight addiction.

Mujica further worked hard to reduce poverty in Uruguay, introducing a minimum wage and boosting welfare programs. He improved the reach of healthcare coverage and committed greater funds to schools, bringing greater technology to education institutions.

The former President's success is rooted in his generosity; his legacy within Uruguay is of someone who had a belief in being kind to people. He refused material benefits for himself and instead dedicated himself to improving the lives of others who truly needed the help. Mujica's story demonstrates that, even in the highest level of government, it's possible to live a generous life and to make a difference in the world.

THE SKILLED
VETERAN CORPS

In March 2011, a magnitude 9.0 earthquake and tsunami struck the Fukushima Daiichi nuclear power plant in Japan. The impact of the tsunami and earthquake was devastating, releasing a colossal number of nuclear materials into the environment. All nuclear plants in Japan were temporarily shut down, and 150,000 residents were forced to evacuate Fukushima. The incident had huge ramifications globally. It brought into question the safety of using nuclear power in its current form, shifting attention away from the energy source; as well as this, concerns are ever-present over the long-term health ramifications for citizens in the wake of the disaster.

An unfair catastrophe though it may have been, the citizens around the power plant were not all content with fleeing. A group of pensioners, totaling more than 400 in number, decided that they needed to contribute to the clean-up effort. The group called themselves the Skilled Veterans Corps, with all members being retired engineers or other professionals aged 60 or older. The pensioners have volunteered to clean up the radioactive fallout surrounding Fukushima, knowing full well that this could bring about fatal health complications.

Their logic is that acute radiation poisoning and other radiation-related illnesses take time to settle in and cause serious damage. The group maintains that by the time the radiation is harming them, they'll be at the end of their lives anyway. Yasuteru Yamada, the group's founder, laid out this idea in a press conference, pleading with his country's politicians:

> "*I am 72 and on average I probably have 13 to 15 years left to live... Even if I were exposed to radiation, cancer could take 20 or 30 years or longer to develop. Therefore, us older ones have less chance of getting cancer.*"

The group's assistance was initially refused by the government. But as time went on, and the power plant continued to spew toxic radioactive material into the surrounding 12.5-mile radius, pressure mounted to allow the pensioners to work.

In the end, Mr. Yamada helped redesign the reactor for the power plant and some volunteers were involved with the cleanup. But the group didn't get the chance to work so the youth wouldn't have to. Many young people have developed serious health conditions from the ongoing cleanup, but the offer from the Skilled Veterans Corps shows the selflessness many of us may not be able to muster. To know that the work is dangerous, life-threatening even, yet volunteering regardless takes a lot of heart, and a lot of belief in the need for your work.

DISPLAYING TRUE HUMAN SPIRIT, EVEN WHEN COMPETING

During the 2016 Olympic Games held in Rio de Janeiro, Brazil, fans were provided with one of the most memorable and heartwarming moments in the history of the competition. The women's 5000m race, a grueling combination of endurance and speed, attracted a vast audience, with millions tuning in via TV and the internet. Shortly after the 3,000m mark, two racers, Abbey D'Agostino and Nikki Hamblin, collided on the track. The collision sent them both tumbling to the ground and the crowd watched on aghast.

The two runners lay on the ground, the other athletes speeding away from them, every second reducing their chances of qualifying for the final. D'Agostino, from America, rose first and rather than attempt to catch up to the pack, stooped and helped Hamblin to her feet. Hamblin, from New Zealand, gingerly gained her composure, and the two limped onward, spurred on by the cheering crowd.

D'Agostino's knee buckled twice further along the track, and she collapsed once more in agony. Hamblin stopped, crouching alongside D'Agostino, patiently waiting for her to regain her composure. The two repeatedly exchanged encouraging words, urging each other to finish the race; each would not allow the other to give in. Both racers finished the race.

The display was difficult to watch. Both runners were clearly in physical agony as well as emotional turmoil. They had given everything to be in the race in the first place but were willing to set aside their own goals in the name of cooperation. The women were hailed as inspirational role models by spectators, and they were given places in the final, due to the irregularity of the events that had taken place.

Regrettably, D'Agostino's injuries were too serious to allow her to compete in the final, but Hamblin did, finishing in 11th place. The lack of a medal wasn't what mattered, however. Their determination, selflessness, and support remained an inspiring image of the Olympic Games for athletes and non-athletes alike. No matter how competitive you are, there's room for compassion and friendship always.

The founder of the modern-day Olympic Games, Pierre de Coubertin, said the spirit of the Olympian is not in victory.

"The most important thing in the Olympic Games is not winning but taking part..., the essential thing in life is not conquering but fighting well."

He would have been proud of D'Agostino and Hamblin's achievements in 2016. They embody what it means to be a true Olympian.

TEDDY'S BEST
WORST BIRTHDAY

There's not much that's more upsetting than seeing a child unhappy. For adults, it may evoke memories of the all-encompassing feeling of being let down at that age, and how much it hurts. Other children, may empathize, wishing they could do something to remove the feelings.

It was this exact motivation that momentarily made Teddy Mazzini a viral sensation in 2018 when a picture was taken of him at his birthday party. His mum had booked the venue for 40 people, 30 classmates and ten adults, but only Teddy and his parents arrived.

His mother, Sil, was distraught at the letdown in numbers. She says that one parent phoned to explain that they weren't going to be able to make it, but every other invitee was AWOL. Teddy seemed unperturbed by the lack of numbers (something that many adults would struggle to cope with); he was happy to spend time with his father. They played games, ate a *lot* of pizza, and thought about what to do with a cake big enough for 40 people; but Sil remained very upset on behalf of her son.

"He didn't understand it…If that happened to an 11- or 12-year-old, it would be tough.

But he's so young that he's fine."

Her friend told her to take a picture of Teddy on his birthday before venting online. Sil decided that the time was right to do so and posted on Facebook about her frustration at the lack of communication from other parents. The intention was to make a point to other parents that they should phone ahead if plans have changed.

It didn't end there. The post was shared time and time again. Teddy's party was picked up by news stations, who tweeted about it and before they knew it, Teddy was a viral sensation. Millions had heard of the boy whose party was abandoned by his friends and invites poured in to offer help in some way. The family refused all invites for extra parties until the basketball team the Phoenix Suns got in touch.

They offered Teddy VIP tickets to their game against the LA Lakers, which Sil decided may just be worth saying yes to. Teddy met a lot of basketballers that he looked up to, as well as receiving special treatment from the club hospitality staff, and had an amazing end to a troubling birthday.

Sil says she wouldn't post if she was given her time again; she had no idea that it was going to spread so far and become such a big part of her family's life. But it helped spread a message to parents who saw it about being courteous and kind. The journey of the post provided us all with a glimpse into how the internet can be used for the good; even if the good is to just help a boy have a nicer birthday.

CHEF'S WHITES LOOK GOOD AS A SUPERHERO OUTFIT

Picture the scene: you're wandering the streets of a city devastated by an earthquake. Collapsed skyscrapers lie across the shattered landscape, blocking off whole highways like vast, concrete roots. The air is thick with dust. The area you are in is borderline unrecognizable as a neighborhood of joy and bustling commerce. Your stomach rumbles yearningly as, out of the dust clouds, a team of chefs adorned in white, armed with pots and pans, arrive to magic up a wonderful meal on the spot.

This is the World Central Kitchen, a charitable organization that brings quality food to communities in crisis. Celebrity chef José Andrés set the charity up in 2010, in response to the devastating Haiti earthquake that caused widespread destruction and killed somewhere between 100,000 and 200,000 Haitians. The charity helped provide decent meals for Haitians living in affected areas and established an operation that acts as a first responder following a disaster.

The charity also works to educate local chefs to help provide food for those in need following a disaster. They rebuild sustainable food systems, providing methods of transporting the food and setting up community kitchens for use.

World Central Kitchen has become adept at quickly mobilizing in the face of natural disasters. In 2017, Puerto Rico was struck by Hurricane Maria, a devastatingly powerful weather event that caused a massive amount of damage and loss of life. The Kitchen quickly arranged an effective relief program and served up two million meals within one month of their arrival. Another example can be found following Hurricane Dorian in 2019. The organization coordinated a massive relief effort that brought 150,000 meals to the country within a matter of weeks.

The work of the World Central Kitchen has a profound impact on the communities it reaches, restoring some semblance of normal life for people who are facing some of the worst disasters in the world. Whether they're serving up meals after a disaster, or supporting communities and food systems, the organization has proved that the simplest things can make a big difference.

An Insignificant Amount, A Very Significant Act

We can teach an invaluable lesson to children about patience, and financial management, by asking them to save up for something they especially want, so they may buy it themselves. They gain a sense of accomplishment and learn that delaying their own gratification is a worthwhile thing to do. The entire process takes a long time to do and for many parents, they may well end up paying for a good chunk of it anyway.

What's more worth teaching, however, is that money can always be used to feed the soul, not just to buy the latest gadget. In 2015, a seven-year-old boy from Texas called Jack Swanson was saving for an iPad and had managed to bring his total to $20. He was proud of his figure so far and intended to keep going until he reached the necessary amount.

That was until early November when his local community was rocked by a bout of racist vandalism targeting the local mosque, a place of worship for Muslims. Jack sat down with his mother, and they discussed what had happened. Jack said that the offensive acts weren't fair, and the Muslim community didn't deserve to have something precious ruined. He agreed with his mother that the $20 he'd saved so far could do a lot more good, by being donated to help the mosque than by being spent on an iPad.

His donation of $20, of course, doesn't go very far in the adult world. But for Faisal Naeem, a board member of the mosque, the donation meant far more than its financial worth.

"It's 20 bucks, but coming from Jack collecting his pennies it's worth 20 million bucks to me and our community. This gives me hope because this means it's not one versus the other."

Jack received some publicity for his act of kindness, and the donation helped the local community heal. Knowing that the hateful act didn't represent the thoughts of the entire neighborhood helped the Muslim community to begin to move on.

Arsalan Iftikhar, who's known on Twitter as The Muslim Guy, read about Jack's generosity and was touched by the gesture. Arsalan is a human rights lawyer and the editor of *The Islamic*

Monthly Magazine. As such, he holds a significant reputation, particularly within American Muslim communities. He bought Jack a brand-new iPad as a token of his gratitude. Iftikhar also wrote a letter to Jack thanking him for his kindness and informing Jack how Muslims across the country were grateful.

The story is a beautiful message of love and a caring soul that's learned effectively how important it is to show kindness to all in modern society. Even if someone didn't get that message initially, Jack's gesture reached a far bigger audience than the vile vandalism ever could.

THE LAST BLOCKBUSTER

This is a story that will inevitably show some generational divides in the readers. If you were born after the year 2000, then it may go over your head; if you were born before 2000, then the story may bring you a wry smile and a memory you didn't even know you'd lost.

Before the days of Netflix, Amazon Prime, and the billions of other streaming services that spring up every other month in the 2020s, the only option was physically renting movies. This meant going to visit a VHS/DVD rental shop, choosing your movie, paying a few dollars, and taking it home to watch it on your VHS/DVD player at home.

(Vocabulary check: A VHS was a chunky tape that played low-resolution movies. A DVD was a disc that played higher-resolution movies. A VHS/DVD player played these. All of these technologies are now redundant.)

For most people, their chosen rental shop was a place called Blockbuster, which formed a crucial part of home entertainment culture in the 1990s and early 2000s. The company had over 9,000 stores worldwide and stocked a great variety of movies, old and new. The store generally had new releases as well as some more niche options, but it wasn't able to last.

147

As the internet grew, so did its capabilities, and Blockbuster failed to adapt. They famously had the option to purchase Netflix, but turned it down, failing to see how internet streaming would catch on. By 2010, the stores began to close in their thousands, signaling an end to the era of physical media. By 2020, there was one store left.

That store is still open. The store is in Bend, Oregon and is now the last remaining store that operates under the name Blockbuster. It's also one of only three video rental stores still operating in the US, all of which mainly run as tourist attractions. The last store brings in income through sleepovers, which you can book via Airbnb online, and affiliations with local companies, such as a local brewery that released a beer called "The Last Blockbuster" in 2018.

There may be more to come. The store decided to run a commercial during the Super Bowl in 2023, helping their sales increase as well as raising brand awareness. Shortly after the event, visitors to www.blockbuster.com saw a reactivated website with the message, "We are working on rewinding your movie" (a reference to video rentals' requirement that customers rewind their videotapes before returning them or have to pay a fee).

The very last Blockbuster is a tale about the strange love that humans have for nostalgia. It's a unique emotion, to yearn to experience something that you haven't had access to for a long time. For those of us who spent time picking out a movie on

Saturday at Blockbuster, if you get the chance, it may be worth taking a visit to Oregon and walking those aisles one more time.

ASHES TO ASHES, CRUMB TO CRUMB

Wherever you are right now, take a look at everything in your immediate vicinity. Create a list. If you're on a train, you may see seats, floor paneling, advertising, windows, handles for grip, and a man coughing too much. If you're in the right mood, it can be especially pleasing to consider that *someone* made all of the things you can see. A person (or several) designed the individual screws that are holding the floor paneling in place, which was in turn thought up by a separate designer in a different office block. The handles were specially crafted to provide balance to people who are standing on their short journey - how wonderful that someone thought to create them.

When you apply this thought to the rest of your life, you'll see a lot of objects that you're grateful someone put a lot of time into thinking about. None are more divisive than the Pringles can.

For some, the Pringles can has a wonderfully intuitive design that provides the only sensible way to store a potato chip that's shaped as it is. For others, the tube is annoying, and there's no way of getting your hand in past the halfway point without pouring crumbs all over yourself. Which camp are you in?

Regardless, the man you must thank (or curse) is Fredric Baur, who designed the now iconic Pringles can in 1966 and was awarded the patent in 1971. Baur had been tasked with creating a potato chip that wasn't greasy and wouldn't become smashed up in the bag, leading to an unsatisfactory snack experience. Baur worked on the shape, which is called a hyperbolic paraboloid, while another scientist worked on making it taste nice. Either way, the work led to the iconic Pringle, which continues to be a dominant force in the handheld snack industry, mainly because of its uniqueness.

This isn't a story about a man making a tube, however, as mildly pleasing as that is. It's about what happened after that man died. In 2008, Fredric Baur passed away at the age of 89. He had three children and many grandchildren who adored him; they adored him so much in fact, that they were quite happy to carry out one last bizarre request from Fredric.

Fredric was always very proud of his work. And yeah, he designed one of the most iconic foods in the world; he should be proud. So proud was he, that he asked his children to put his ashes into a Pringles can. Larry Baur, the inventor's son, said that the children always found the notion hilarious and very fitting for their father:

> "When my dad first raised the burial idea in the 1980s, I chuckled about it, my siblings and I briefly debated what flavor to use, but I said, 'Look, we need to use the original.'"

A portion of Fredric Baur's ashes were stored in an Original Flavor can and buried in a grave in Springfield Township, Ohio.

Some more went into an urn, to be buried alongside the can, and the rest were given to each of his grandchildren.

Perhaps one day, someone will find the can, hoping to have a delicious snack and instead get a ghost scientist leaping out at them from this piece of iconic food storage.

THE BEST LEMON-AID EVER

Sometimes it's easy to dismiss children. Their untamed imagination shapes their world into an often-unrealistic version that doesn't match up with older people's views. A child sees a grand idea that will make a difference to their community; an adult sees the paperwork, logistics, and potential lawsuits. It's a truism that will forever be at play. Part of our maturing is learning not to be at the mercy of our own minds, and it's perfectly normal to have this dichotomy at play.

But sometimes, a child just comes up with something good. An idea that's either brilliant or sweet, and as adults, we can help make their dream a reality.

This was the case in 2014, in Maple Ridge, British Columbia, when a young boy named Quinn Callander found out his friend needed surgery. Quinn was only seven years old at the time, and he had a friend called Brayden, who was affected by cerebral palsy. Cerebral palsy is a group of neurological disorders affecting movement and coordination caused by brain damage. In Brayden's case, his right arm and leg were dramatically affected, and his ongoing physiotherapy teaching him to walk caused him a great deal of pain.

The surgery proposed was going to cost $20,000 and would have to be carried out in America. The options in Canada were more invasive and risked leaving Brayden wheelchair-bound; the American surgery had great promise in bringing far better movement for the young boy.

Quinn found out about this and was adamant that he should help. Quinn said that he arrived home after he learned of the surgery and told his parents that he wanted to set up a lemonade stand. His parents were wonderfully supportive, praising Quinn for his selfless thinking. They helped him prepare to sell lemonade for his friend. The community around the families found out about the stand and came out in full force to raise money for the life-altering surgery. Local media covered it and helped bring more customers to the boy's stand.

On the side, Quinn's mother knew that $20,000 was unlikely to be made by a lemonade stand by itself, so she set up a GoFundMe. This helped bring more attention to Quinn's efforts, and $24,000 was raised to help Brayden access surgery in America. The story is so heartwarming not just because of Quinn's immediate and natural desire to help, but also because of the adults who rallied around him to ensure his dream became reality. Sometimes, it's worth supporting the children. They see the world a little differently from the grownups.

SAVING HIS LIFE EVEN IF THEY HATE WHAT HE DOES

There exist certain stereotypes about prisoners and prison guards that many people will simply assume are always true. The stereotypes are perpetuated by TV and film, which show guards treating prisoners cruelly and prisoners constantly trying to outsmart or harm the guards. For those of us who have never been in a prison on either side of the bars, this may as well be the absolute truth of life inside. In many institutions, this dynamic probably does play out from time to time, but not in all circumstances.

In 2020, three incarcerated men saved the life of a prison guard who suffered serious injuries while at work. The men (Terry Loveless, Walter Whitehead, and Mitchell Smalls) were in their cells and noticed that the deputy didn't seem quite right at work. The deputy went about his normal procedures but seemed sluggish and generally unwell. They watched him with a cautious eye as he sat down at his desk and fell unconscious. He rolled off the desk and fell to the concrete floor, sustaining a serious head injury.

The roommates immediately sprang to action, pounding against their walls and doors, screaming the deputy's name. The noise spread to the entire unit who joined in the banging and shouting, creating an almighty racket as the deputy lay unresponsive, bleeding. After some time, the deputy heard the noise. It crept into his stirring consciousness as approaching drums and calls of his name. The deputy assumed an inmate was in trouble, so he slowly and shakily got to his feet, pushing the button to open the cell doors.

The inmates sprinted to the deputy, provided care and aid, and encouraged him to relax. They used the phone to call for help from nearby deputies and operated the radio to get the word out that there was an emergency in their unit. Help arrived almost instantly, and the deputy's life was saved. The head injury had caused him to lose a vast amount of blood, and he was not in a good way, but he survived.

The heroic inmates had their pictures taken, and the Gwinnett County Sheriff's Office posted on Facebook to make public their gratitude to the men who had rushed to the aid of the deputy:

> "These inmates came to his aid because our deputy, like most law enforcement officers, treats people with the dignity they deserve. These inmates had no obligation whatsoever to render aid to a bleeding, vulnerable deputy, but they didn't hesitate. Many people have strong opinions about law enforcement officers and criminals, but this incident clearly illustrates the potential goodness found in both."

The post received media attention, along with hundreds of thousands of likes and shares as well-wishers sent their gratitude to the prisoners. The incident demonstrates it doesn't matter if we *seem* to be in opposition to someone, we should always seek to help our fellow human beings if they're in trouble.

WHO COULD HAVE BEEN NUMBER 229?

Have you heard of the phrase "pay it forward" before? The meaning behind it is that you respond to someone's kindness toward you by being kind to someone else. The phrase garnered a great deal of attention on the internet in the early 2010s. Many people thought that if millions of people spread the message, then the world would be a kinder place. If we all took the message to heart, it would be indeed.

This was seen in practice at a drive-thru Tim Horton's in Winnipeg, Canada in 2013.

T'was the season to be jolly, only a few days before Christmas, and a customer was collecting their order at the popular fast-food establishment. They reached over to pay for their food and said to the cashier that they would pay for the person behind them as well. The unknown customer was thanked for their generosity, and they disappeared into the night, like a very kind Batman.

They couldn't have predicted what would happen in their wake.

The lucky customer who now had some free donuts and a coffee (or whatever else they may have ordered; the wraps can be quite nice) seemed to get the message. They told the cashier that they'd like to pay for the person behind them. You can see where this is going - the next customer did the same, then the next, and so on, and so on.

In-store customers caught wind of what had been happening in the drive-thru and jumped in to pay for the person behind them in the queue. The atmosphere developed into a giving frenzy, with the manager proudly announcing how long the "chain" was. The number soared past 100 orders quickly and above 150 as customers looked on beaming at the collective, spontaneous generosity on display.

In the end, they paid 228 orders forward. A remarkable feat, once again reinforcing stereotypes about Canadians as being generally kind people. Yet as with anything, not everyone is on the same page. On order 229, a man staunchly refused to pay for the next customer's three coffees after he had received four free coffees. Of course, we don't know that person's circumstances; perhaps the money was truly needed and the gift made a big difference to their Christmas. Perhaps they simply didn't like giving, who knows?

We don't think about customer 229, we think about the 228 people who kept a beautiful act of generosity flowing in the lead-up to the most wonderful time of the year. Perhaps you could start the next one?

A BIRD IN THE HAND
IS WORTH $20M

If you're unfamiliar with Brian Blessed, the booming, brash, and bold English actor, then you may want to quickly Google him. Blessed is now in his mid-80s and is still as passionate about his craft as he has ever been. He's acted alongside the very best, starring in TV and film across six decades, and has innumerable stories to prove it.

Blessed is also known for his, quite frankly, bonkers tales outside of acting. Among many stories that could be written in this book that meet the category of "happy" or "uplifting" include:

- The time he helped a woman give birth
- When an orangutan rowed him down the Amazon
- His hunting of the Yeti
- Climbing Mount Everest

The list goes on. But one story that is both hilarious and tells us a lot about childhood innocence and bravado comes from when Blessed was 12, growing up in Sheffield, UK.

It was post-World War II, in the aftermath of unimaginable death and destruction across the planet, and Blessed was attending a World Peace Conference in Sheffield with some of his friends. These conferences aimed to show beauty, art, music, and cooperation so people may keep peace close to their hearts.

Blessed and his friends found their way to a secret area where some performers and famous faces were gathered. There he saw singers he admired and a man who seemed to be signing autographs; everyone appeared keen to meet him. Blessed had heard that the man was Pablo Picasso, one of the world's most well-known and celebrated artists.

Blessed was unimpressed. He was adamant that the man was not Picasso. He approached him and said:

"If you're Picasso, draw me something!"

Picasso observed this small boy with amusement and told Blessed that he would draw him a dove of peace. Within 30 seconds, he'd presented the small (but uninterested) boy with a drawing of a dove. The image didn't just show a dove, though. If you changed your perspective, it also showed a hand reaching out. This signified the necessity of peace in the post-war era, with a general tone of love and humanity within the drawing. It's beautiful. Blessed, however, was not impressed.

"That's not a dove! I'll draw you a dove!"

Blessed threw the picture on the floor. It was presented at the conference later and now hangs in Sheffield Gallery, valued somewhere between £20m and £50m (US $26–64m).

Brian finds the whole story very funny and reflects that for a child, certain perspectives on life and art just aren't yet available.

It is only as adults that we see the true grace and beauty behind such things. It's something to bear in mind next time we become frustrated at younger generations not understanding something or being seemingly apathetic about aspects of life adults may love. They may not understand it when they're children, but they may understand it when they're in their twenties - and isn't that more beautiful?

Having said that, don't let your child throw a drawing worth millions of pounds on the floor.

THE THIRD ACT'S ALWAYS
THE BEST ANYWAY

There's a misconception unhelpfully adopted in our world that after a certain age, people lose their spark and their usefulness. Think about what your first impression is when you hear the phrase "old person." Is it to imagine an elderly woman pottering about her house? Is it an old man asleep in his armchair? These stereotypes are very unhelpful, and none of us would want to be thought of as being on the wind-down in our lives.

The notion of the Third Act has been spreading in certain circles, as greater numbers of people change careers or switch up their lives after the age of 45 and find a newer, greater purpose. The following is a story from the book *The Third Act: Reinventing Your Next Chapter* by Josh Sapan, the message of which is that life isn't over because you're not 18. There's always time for a change.

John Kerr worked for 40 years at WGBH, a broadcasting company. He enjoyed his work very much, but it wasn't what he *wanted* to do when he was a child. He'd wanted to be a fireman or a park ranger because of the hats they wear. He retired from broadcasting, with no hat, at the age of 65. There was no goal in mind for his retirement, no hobby he wanted to chase, nor any part-time job he had his eye on. After spending a few weeks thinking, Kerr decided to drive his camper van to go and visit family in Wyoming, which took him through the famous Yellowstone National Park.

Yellowstone National Park is America's first national park and holds a special place in many people's hearts. The vast acres of land and thousands of animals that can be found populating it bring joy to the millions who visit it every year. While there, Kerr found that the Yellowstone Park Foundation was looking to hire people, to help teach tourists about wolves.

Kerr's daughter told him to go for it, so he did. Signing on as an intern, he learned all he could about educating people in the park. He stood out; most other interns were high school or college students, looking for a bit of money. Kerr was different in ways other than his age as well. His passion drove him to succeed in this brand-new field. He'd always had a love for the great outdoors ever since his childhood spent on adventures with his grandfather. He's been ready for this his whole life.

Kerr felt that he wanted to do something that had more of an impact. His education ensures that people are safe around animals. He helps with medical emergencies and treasures his role in assisting to keep the beautiful Yellowstone National Park sacred. He's now the park ranger he dreamed of becoming as a child.

The point is that millions of people feel the "call" between the ages of 45 to 70 years old, this sense that they want to do something else. Perhaps their career is unfulfilling, or a dream has been left out to dry for too long. It's never too late to give it a go.

It's not only a message for those in that age bracket. It's also a message for young people who are in a hurry to get stuck into a career quickly. It doesn't matter if you have always wanted to do..., if it's not how you imagined, then move on. There are a lot of ways to spend your time while earning a living, and they're not all exactly what you might have planned.

CONCLUSION

You've reached the end, congratulations!

These stories were designed to bring a bit of optimism and happiness to you. Our modern life is full of sad tales and unfortunate circumstances; it can serve us well to remember that there remain plenty of happy and kind acts happening all around us.

Some of the stories will, hopefully, have inspired you. Whether it's the spontaneous act of buying a stranger a coffee, standing up to corruption, or raising money for your friend who's having a hard time, you can take the messages from these into your everyday life. Aim to spread the joy like these people (or penguins) have done. If you do so, it won't only improve everyone else's life, but yours as well.

A recent study conducted by the University of California found that people are healthier and happier if they're able to provide charity and kindness to others. We can do this by reaching out to friends, family, and people we've never met before. If you spot a GoFundMe page to help raise money for a good cause, ask yourself if the extra snacks that your $10 could buy can be used better.

Perhaps you didn't find anything inspiring, which is fine as well. Perhaps for a small book of short stories, that aim is a little far-fetched. If the book was able to make you smile, however, or if you had a light-hearted chuckle at the sillier stories, then that's enough.

Either way, no matter what your opinion has been of the book, please take the time to slow yourself down and be kind to other people. You might just find yourself in the next edition of 72 inspiring short stories, and if you don't, then you'll at least have made someone's life a little bit better.

Comedian Tim Minchin put it best, in his address to UWA in 2013:

"You never know where you might end up. Just be aware the next worthy pursuit will probably appear in your periphery, which is why you should be careful of long-term dreams. If you focus too far in front of you, you won't see the shiny thing out the corner of your eye."

Printed in Great Britain
by Amazon

43378294R00096